I CAN, YOU CAN

Rania Habib

Conscious Dreams
P U B L I S H I N G

This book is not intended as a substitute for the medical advice of physicians. The reader should regularly consult a physician in matters relating to their health, particularly with respect to any symptoms that may require diagnosis or medical attention.

Published by Conscious Dreams Publishing
www.consciousdreamspublishing.com

Book Consultant Daniella Blechner

Edited by Elise Abram

Typeset by Oksana Kosovan

ISBN: 978-1-917584-32-6

For my brother

I hope you can say that you chose your life and didn't settle for it.

Contents

CHAPTER I

Whispers of Unexpected Grief

'Trust that still, small voice that says,
"This might work, and I'll try it."'

Diane Mariechild

I want to tell you about my voice, the one that whispers deep inside me, the one only I can hear. She is my compass, my guide, the quiet force that tells me what's right and what's wrong, when to stay and when to leave. She is the one who urges me to say yes when everything inside me trembles and to say no when the world insists I comply. Sometimes, her words are crystal clear, ringing in my ears like a bell. Other times, she's barely a murmur, lost in the noise of life. But there is one truth she's never let go of: *there is more to life than the one I am living right now.*

I didn't understand what that meant at the time, but I knew, deep in my bones, that one day—*one day*— I would unleash all the creativity and potential that had been silently brewing within me for so long. I knew that, at some point, I would look back and understand everything she had been trying to tell me. But until then—until I knew how, or when, or even *why*—I just swayed through life like a leaf caught in the wind. I made the best of the bad days and took the bad with the good. I wasn't truly alive; I merely existed, boxed in by a reality that felt prewritten for me, while my voice inside grew louder, demanding to be heard as I grew older.

As a young girl, books were my escape, though I wasn't like most kids who found solace in fiction. From the age of 11, I found myself drawn to self-development books and convinced my parents to buy them for me. I wasn't a child prodigy or a genius by any stretch of the imagination, so my understanding of those books was simple at best. I mostly grasped the general idea of what the author was trying to convey, but the deeper meanings often eluded me. Back then, if I came across a word I didn't understand—especially one with five syllables—I had to dust off my antiquated paperback dictionary and sift through its pages. But as an 11-year-old, I rarely had the patience for that, so my comprehension was a bit... basic. Still, even at that young age, something in those books spoke to me, something I would only fully understand much later in life.

As I entered adolescence, I began taking myself to the bookstore, and there was an almost magnetic pull towards the self-development section. Even with a blindfold on, I'd have found my way there. I didn't always know what to do with the information I read, but I was deeply aware that I wanted to embody at least a fraction of the qualities, behaviours and wisdom that leapt off those pages. They spoke to a version of me I wasn't yet but could feel stirring inside. Little did I know that the journey I was about to embark on would be nothing like the one I had imagined.

On the 25th of April 2016, my brother died. He was 21 years old. We were two years, four months, and 20 days apart.

My brother and I were the only siblings in our family, but we were more than that: we were best friends. Anyone who knew us could see it. He was the kind of person who would give you everything, even if it was the last of what he had: his last dime, his last bite or his last ounce of energy. He had a way of making me laugh a little louder, smile a little bigger and feel a little brighter. He would listen to you as though the world had paused and, in his eyes, you were the only person who mattered in that moment, and you could feel it in the quiet reverence with which he heard every word. His heart was a reservoir of forgiveness, flowing endlessly so that even before the next beat of your heart, any wrong was already forgotten. His mind resembled a garden untouched by time, one where the rarest of flowers bloomed: patience, empathy and compassion. He lived as if generosity was woven into the very fabric of his soul; each word, each gesture and each action was an offering without limits. He was, in every sense, every beautiful word you could find in the dictionary and more.

On the evening of the 24th of April 2016, everything felt simple, almost ordinary. We went out for pizza, laughter filling the air as we savoured the warm, familiar comfort of a shared bite. I remember feeling so full afterwards, satisfied in the way only a good meal can leave you. When he dropped me off at home, it seemed like a quiet, perfect end to a calm evening. The world was right. Everything was fine.

But then the next day came, and he never returned.

Hours bled into each other, the empty space left by his absence growing more profound with each passing hour. At first, I told myself there was an explanation, some reasonable cause, a delay, or a misunderstanding, but the longer I waited, the more those explanations faded like wisps of smoke dissolving in the wind. He'd never not come home; that wasn't his usual behaviour. What had started as confusion shifted, slowly but relentlessly, into something far darker: worry. I replayed that night over and over, searching for any clue, any detail that might hold the key to where he was.

Later that same day, a knock at the door came. It felt... sharp. Two men stood there, their black suits seeming to absorb the dimming light around them. They didn't speak at first, but their badges gleamed coldly in the fading evening sun. Their faces were unreadable masks of professionalism, but their presence carried a weight that seemed to press down on me. They asked to come inside. Their voices were smooth and steady but there was something about the formality of their tone that set every nerve on edge. They stepped over the threshold, gently telling me I needed to go upstairs while they spoke with my parents. I remember the quiet urgency in their words, but it didn't truly hit me until I was alone, sitting at the top of the stairs: something had happened. In that hollow silence, the seconds stretching into eternity before they could bring themselves to speak, I felt it. I felt that in a matter of minutes, everything I had ever known, life as I once knew it, would fracture irreparably.

He died. The words came slowly as if the very air couldn't bear to speak them. And in that instant, time seemed to stretch. Everything froze, then slammed back into motion, crashing apart in a blur of disbelief. The world around me fractured into pieces and with it, any sense of reality. It was as if the ground itself had turned to dust beneath me. I never could have prepared for the weight of that moment. No language could capture the weight of the world falling upon you all at once.

It was an arson attack, a phrase I didn't even understand until that day. At the time, it felt like the worst kind of cruel irony that a word could be so distant, so foreign, until it became the very thing that consumed your life. Arson meant the evidence had been destroyed. It meant that hope, any sliver of it, was gone. It meant there was no chance of survival. The flames had taken everything. Why? Why him? Why like that? The answer was unknown, and that unknown will linger with me forever.

When he died, a heavy-hearted, self-destructive and angry-at-life teenager emerged from the carefree, wildly ambitious and happy-go-lucky girl I once was. In that moment, my light flickered out. The world around me seemed to freeze. No sensation, no colour, no yesterday, no tomorrow. Just an overwhelming silence. Grief swallowed everything. Every path I tried to take, every desperate attempt to escape, only led me deeper into the thick fog where there was no fresh air to be found. Not a single soul knew just how dark it had become. I lost all sense of who I was, and in that lost space, friendships faded away and weekends were spent alone, curled up in bed for what felt like an eternity. The voice in my head was still there, but it was a whisper now, barely audible over the suffocating weight of everything I was trying to outrun.

I lived what you might call a 'normal' life until the 25th of April 2016. I was 19, gearing up to sit my first set of law exams at university, but on that day, everything changed. The tragedy that had struck my family quickly spread across countless news channels, both nationally and internationally. The media, the public, the community—everyone watched. In the span of just a few hours, my home no longer felt like home. It was transformed into a media circus. I went from being a grieving teenage girl to the face of my family's pain, a voice for the world, a messenger for something no one should ever have to speak of. The girl who had only ever used her voice for a small circle of people suddenly found herself speaking to hundreds—thousands—as the weight of her grief became a public spectacle.

The world heard my voice for the very first time, but the doors to my soul were shrouded by the silicone sunglasses I used to hide my tear-streaked eyes for seven long years.

I used to dread the start of every week as though it was the very first Monday I'd ever known. When it was hot, I complained about the places that weren't cool. When it rained, it seemed like it was never-ending. I didn't hate life; I just didn't know how to live it fully. I became a shadow of who I was, someone who tried to blend in, take up less space and avoid risk at all costs.

Years later, on the 7th of November 2021, I reached a breaking point. I refused to let grief continue to cripple my life any longer. In the midst of my pain, something inside me shifted—a light bulb moment—though I still can't fully explain it. It was as if a spark had been waiting to be ignited. I suddenly saw that there was more to life than retreating into darkness and drowning in sorrow. I realised that I only had *one* life, and for the first time in years, I wondered what I was actually doing with it.

Nothing.

In that moment, I knew I needed to do something. Nobody was going to come to rescue me. Only I could save myself.

Sometimes, you find yourself lost in the middle of nowhere, and other times, in that very nowhere, you find out exactly who you are. That's what happened to me. For a long time, I sealed my eyes shut, unwilling to let myself glimpse any trace of joy. How could I, without my brother? In my world, it felt impossible, but one day, just for a split second, I forgot why I was so consumed by anger and pain, and I dared to look. It was only a brief glance, but when you've been in the darkness for so long, even a fleeting peek at the light feels like a blinding flood.

They say that just before you die, your whole life flashes before your eyes. In that moment, I understood. I saw every stage, every cycle, every season, every single memory of my life magnified and slowed down as though the universe was giving me a chance to truly see. I used to feel so helpless, like a child who couldn't fend for herself, but I couldn't have been more wrong. Children aren't helpless; they're magic. Somewhere along the way, we teach them to dull and bury that magic.

I don't know what happened to me, but when I lost everything, I finally found my magic, and in that moment, I knew it was time to break free, to explore the vibrant tapestry of a new reality, one full of colour, possibility and life.

The distress that had once consumed my mind and body had also taught me to shrink within limitations. It told me that not much would change for me, that bad things were inevitable and that I would always be weighed down by them. I used to hear the advice, but I didn't truly listen. I would engage but only half-heartedly, distracted by my own misery. I became attached to sadness, rejecting the very help and guidance that was offered to me. Even when others showed me the way, I couldn't bring myself to follow. I was given attention, but I couldn't understand the depth of it.

Over time, I realised that no one could save me but myself. I had to become someone entirely new to create a life that felt different and meaningful, so I made a choice, a quiet but powerful one. I opened myself up, slowly and carefully, to kinder beliefs about who I was and what the world could be. I learnt to soften my heart and trust in the process, even when it felt uncertain or as if I might fall. Most of all, I learnt to be patient with myself, knowing that change wasn't instant and growth didn't always follow a straight path. But I was ready to stay the course, no matter how many times it seemed to take a step back.

I started by detoxing my body, cleansing my gut before I could even begin to listen to it. Next, I tackled the clutter in my bedroom, throwing out years of accumulated junk. As I sifted through the mess, I stumbled upon a stack of self-help books buried beneath my bed like an overcrowded Turkish bazaar. I hoped that would be the turning point I was waiting for, but instead, they felt like an endless loop of generic advice that just didn't resonate. What I craved was the raw, unfiltered truth, something real, something that truly spoke to me, so I made a promise to myself: when I emerged from the darkness, I would write the book that captured the raw reality of what really worked today, not another self-help title on the shelf.

I wrote this book because life has a way of sweeping you up in unexpected adventures, often taking away the most precious gifts you hold, but I want to remind you that through every trial, you will find peace when grief enters your life and you will discover your inner strength when the world tells you 'no'.

Loss came to my family like a thief in the night, as it does for so many around the world. It doesn't always come in the form of death—it takes many shapes and seasons. There is the loss of family and friendships, marriages and unions, material possessions and finances, memory, health, body weight—list goes on. If you live on this Earth, you are almost certain to face some form of loss. We're never truly prepared for it, but once it touches your life, it changes you forever. There's no manual, guide or degree that can navigate you through the inevitable journey of loss, no clear path back from grief to abundance, from sorrow to strength, so I wrote one for you based on the principles that truly worked for me.

When people asked if I had any siblings after my brother died, I would say, 'No,' not because it was true but because I didn't know how else to answer. What was once a simple, familiar response had become foreign, like I was fumbling for a response that didn't exist anymore. It was as if the word 'brother' had lost its shape, no longer fitting into the space it used to occupy, but with time and a kind of quiet clarity I couldn't have understood or seen back then: death doesn't sever bonds. To put it more plainly, death doesn't end relationships. They stretch across time, slipping past the boundaries of the visible world, surviving in the spaces we can't see but still feel, like the smell that lingers in a room long after someone has left.

While he was alive in body, he'd taught me how to live with loss, shown me, not in words but in the very way he lived, that love didn't fade with death. He was everything I needed to know about strength, about holding sorrow without being consumed by it, about how to move through grief without letting it define me. Even now, in his absence, I realise that the lessons he left me are woven into my everyday, like an invisible thread still connecting us.

Through life, death and all the beautiful moments in between, I've learnt the importance of never letting the flicker within me fade. Even in the darkest moments when hope feels distant, life must continue. You'll make it through to the other side. You might not emerge the same as you were before, but you'll definitely be transformed, polished, wiser and more resilient than before.

I hope my book inspires you the way my own journey has lit a fire within me, a fire I never knew I was capable of sparking. No matter how dark the tunnel may seem, there will always be a light waiting for you at the end.

This isn't a sob story; it's a message of hope and encouragement. I write from a place of deep privilege, grateful for the opportunity to share my truth, to speak from my heart. Seven years later, I finally took off the sunglasses that had kept me in the dark, and I realised my journey had been bittersweet but essential. What I needed all along wasn't a perfect path but the unwavering support of my soul's voice, guiding me through it all.

CHAPTER 2

Where Mind and Heart Lead, Plans Follow

Every blade of grass has its Angel that bends over it and whispers, 'Grow, grow.'

The Talmud

For a long time, I believed that my happiness was tied to my law degree, so I threw myself into my studies and worked tirelessly day and night. Whilst I deeply valued the education I received, I soon realised that it wasn't enough to bring me the fulfilment and sense of purpose I longed for. For some, a law degree might provide all the purpose they needed, and that was perfectly valid, but for me, I felt a calling for something more, something beyond the pages of textbooks and legal briefs. I wanted to do more than just handle cases; I wanted to reach out and touch the hearts of those who needed to hear my voice. The three years I spent at university after my brother's death were incredibly uncomfortable. Grief had stirred something deep within me, a quiet, undeniable knowing that my true purpose wasn't to spend my life studying law but to make a meaningful, lasting impact on the world. Every day, I felt the weight of that knowing pulling me toward a future that was different from the one I had planned.

I believe the hardships I faced taught me more than any academic pursuit ever could. Had I not gone through those challenges, would I have had the drive to transform my life? I suppose I'll never know.

My inner voice and imagination acted like a magnet, keeping my faith alive that a happier life was possible. Meditation guided me towards a life free from anxiety, gently holding me in place and reminding me not to abandon my dreams just yet. I made it my responsibility to make my mind a kinder and happier place before waiting for anything in my life to change. I stopped relying on external plans I believed would bring me happiness and chose instead to shift my state of consciousness. At every crossroads, I chose to love without limits, chose happiness without conditions, chose kindness without hesitation and chose abundance without boundaries. Most importantly, I chose to believe in my own potential. Through every choice and decision, I rewired my baseline to one of happiness and limitless possibility.

After experiencing grief, my subconscious mind became wired to believe that I could only grow within certain limits. It told me I could surpass what previous generations had achieved but only to a point, not enough to reach the level of freedom I instinctively knew possible. There was always a ceiling, just enough to prove myself but not enough to break free. The more I connected with my inner voice, the more I believed my dreams were attainable, and I realised that if I didn't reprogram my mind, it would keep me trapped in mediocrity.

Your mind and character open more doors than your hands ever will. They will take you further than any talent, guiding you into spaces your intelligence can't reach. Together, they serve as your business card, your ticket to the top and your marketer. They determine how much or how little opportunity you receive. This goes before anything you try to do, any plan you try to follow, and anything you try to attain. It's not a cryptic message to decode but an invitation to approach life as a giver, to expand, to add value, and to serve the greater good of both yourself and humanity. Your mind and character should not be conditioned by expectations or transactions; they should come unconditionally without any strings attached, reflecting the truth of who you really are. When you give without expectations, you remain grounded in love, unaffected by hate. Each moment presents a choice: to love or to hate. Every time you choose love, you pave the way for a life of abundance and connection. Your mind is the force that will carry you through the world, so the best investment you can make is in yourself.

The golden rule is simple: the opportunities you encounter are directly aligned with how well you've met yourself. Perhaps you need to be kinder to open the door to greater opportunities. Maybe you need to approach others with more love than frustration to unlock new possibilities. It's possible that showing more grace to the strangers you pass could lead to the connections you've been waiting for. A kind heart can propel you forward by years, bypassing dead-end paths, and a simple smile or a gentler tone can be the catalyst for the fresh start you've been longing for. These acts may seem small, but they are, in fact, the most significant moments in life. If you aren't aligning with your goals, it's because you haven't yet met yourself deeply enough.

If you're not where you'd like to be, don't be hard on yourself. Without this current mindset, you won't be able to experience or master the next phase. Instead, gently tell yourself, 'Thank you for all you've done, but in order for me to move forward, I need to leave you behind.' I wrote *I Can You Can* after navigating chaotic and unfamiliar life experiences that ultimately brought me to this point.

Remember, true expansion cannot happen without embracing the mess, clutter, difficult relationships and risk.

If you're sitting here today haunted by the thought, *If only I knew then what I know now,* take a deep breath and remember this: you didn't. And that's not a failure; it's a part of your story. The pain, the heartache, the wrong turns—they weren't mistakes. They were the fire that shaped you, the struggle that forged the strength you carry today. You couldn't have done it any other way. It had to happen that way, even when it felt like the world was crumbling beneath you.

The truth is, *you can't judge yesterday with today's eyes.* If you do, you'll be chained to regret, paralysed by what could have been. And that shame, that feeling of 'I should have known better' will only drag you down, weighing on you like an anchor. But here's the gift: that pain wasn't in vain. It's the very reason you stand where you do now, with wisdom that can *only* come from surviving, learning and living.

So, stop punishing yourself for the choices you made when you didn't know what you know now. Those choices were stepping stones, and without them, you wouldn't be who you are. Trust that everything, even the hardest parts, was meant to unfold exactly as it did. And now, with this new knowledge, you can rise.

Before we move on, I want you to know that abundance isn't something we create; it's always present. What we do create are the limitations we place on ourselves. Every day, there is abundant opportunity to be patient, to be courageous, to be loving, and to go after what you truly want. The choice is always yours, and sometimes, we simply choose otherwise.

Your mind and character are your who-am-I. They come before any plans you've ever made. No strategy will succeed if you don't first love yourself and your soul. Until you shift your mind to truly believe you can, you won't be able to.

Let me remind you: if you have a mind, you have a genius mind. Be mindful of your thoughts, for they are your commands. Throughout this journey, remember that no one else is you. We don't get multiple chances at life; we only have this one.

CHAPTER 3

The Silent Currents That Carry Us Forward

'You can cut all the flowers, but you cannot keep spring from coming.'

Pablo Neruda

During my journey of self-recovery, I spent hours searching for something—anything—to comfort me. As you read on, you might think this is obvious, but when you're deep in the throes of pain, it's the last thing on your mind. Here's what I discovered.

Antoine Laurent Lavoisier, father of chemistry and the founder of the First Law of Thermodynamics: the Law of Conservation of Energy, said, 'Nothing is lost, nothing is created, everything is transformed.'[1]

What did Lavoisier mean?

The primal matter and components—every ingredient, every portion, all factors and details that created our universe—have always existed in one form or another. Nothing has never not been here.

Einstein also tells us, 'Energy cannot be created or destroyed; rather, it can only be changed from one form to another.'[2]

---

1 *Lavoisier, A.L. (1774/2023, July 13). Nothing is lost, nothing is created, everything is transformed. Elevate Society. https://el-evatesociety.com/nothing-is-lost-nothing-is/*

2 *Quoted in Mohan, S. (2020, May 24). Energy cannot be created or destroyed. LinkedIn. https://www.linkedin.com/pulse/ energy-cannot-created-destroyed-shiv-mohan-ceng-mba-pmp-mirse/*

Here, Einstein meant that nothing ever dies, dissipates or vanishes, nor is it ever lost. Everything is only an intertwined and continual affair of transformation.

The entirety of your life is energy: your consciousness, your feelings, your thoughts and your disposition. We aren't just solid matter; we are more than what meets the eye. You are welcomed into your body the moment you leave your mother's womb, but that doesn't mean you die when the body dies; *no*, we are more than just our bodies. We are the perpetuation of endless longevity. We have been carried on and on. We are transformed extensions of our ancestors and descendants. We are born, bred and contain a spark of the whole universe within us because nothing is ever destroyed.

If you believe in the Big Bang, then believe that we are not a product of it but still in the process of it.

I had another 'light bulb' moment: if everything is always in a state of transformation, then surely I could transform my pain into something else, something worth living for, something better than my past, something new. I spent so long chasing a light I couldn't reach, trying to escape or destroy my pain, but when I read about transformation, I realised I had been approaching it all wrong. In that moment, I thought, 'Why not give it a try? What's the worst that could happen?' So, 'Transform, not destroy' became my new inner mantra. From that point on, grief became something far more valuable to me: an experience of transformation. All it took was becoming aware of my energy. Slowly but surely, I began to open myself up to possibility. The door to happiness, which had been shut for so long, creaked open, and with it, the accumulated weight of past pain slowly dissolved into the air.

The reward for becoming conscious was healing.

CHAPTER 4

Disrupting Abundance

"It's a funny thing about life; if you refuse to accept anything but the best, you very often get it."

Somerset Maugham

It's time for me to disrupt your definition of abundance.

Abundance has always been more than the balance in your bank account. It extends far beyond material wealth.

Abundance is an energy woven into your relationships, your happiness, your health, your opportunities, your spirituality, your food, your limits and your potential. It surrounds us in ways we often turn a blind eye to every day, but today, let's remember and see abundance for what it truly is.

Abundance is in the people you smile at, the size of your smile and how often you share it. It's the kindness you offer, no matter how many times others reject it. Abundance is the vast sky that lights your path. It's the countless blades of grass filling the world's cracks, the invisible pollen drifting through the air.

Abundance is found in both your milestones and your micro-moments, in every way you use the resources available to you. It's knowing that when things don't go as planned, it's still the perfect outcome. Whether it comes with a divorce, an eviction or mounting debt, it may feel heavy or light, tearful or heart-shattering, but it is always perfect.

Abundance demands that you be so convicted, so ignited, so fierce and devoted that you never question the journey it takes you on. The only consequence of abundance is that every moment, every path, and every destination is as perfect and abundant as it should be. Your mind cannot fathom lack.

Your level of conviction to live an abundant life will show the next time you take action. If abundance doesn't move you more deeply than it did before, then you're not fully convicted yet.

When you recognise the fullness of abundance that surrounds you, it will push you to do things you've never done before. It will urge you to become the person you've always wanted to be. It will push you to speak the words you've been holding back and take the actions you've been avoiding. The truth will reveal the urgency to step into your true self because once you do, you'll see yourself more clearly than ever before. This is not a time to ask for permission; it's a time to step forward, give notice and serve the purpose you came here to fulfil.

Our planet has every resource, every bit of wealth and all the reserves needed for everything that has been and ever will be accomplished. When you expand the expression of who you are, you signal to the universe that abundance can be reflected in the expansion you're willing to offer. If you define your current life by the lack of abundance you perceive around you, you're giving the universe the exact verdict you expect it to deliver. All you need to do is redefine, relate to and believe in abundance differently than you currently do.

If creation is abundant, then so are you. You were created with exactly what you need to create more of what you desire. At every moment, you will always have what you need, even if you don't believe it right now.

So:

WHEN YOU LEARN TO DO MORE WITH LESS, YOU WILL BE ABLE TO DO LESS AND CREATE MORE.

Try it.

When I fully understood what it meant to be an author without lacking any part of that concept or its expression, and when I realised I could call myself an author with nothing more than a pencil and a scrap of printer paper, I discovered how to create more with less and take my idea of authorship to a whole new level.

When you recognise that you are abundant in every moment, knowing you can achieve what you need with what you currently have, you will empower yourself in ways you never imagined. By doing more with less, you'll invigorate your spirit and unlock the potential to open new doors.

For this to work, you must first open the doors of your imagination. Understand that, as you are right now, with nothing more than what you already have, you are fully capable of accomplishing what you need. Once I stopped measuring, comparing, and doubting myself, thinking that because all I had was a pencil and a scrap of printer paper, I couldn't be the author I dreamed of, I finally became the author I was meant to be.

DISRUPTING ABUNDANCE II

Societal systems weren't designed to serve us but rather to keep us serving them. We're trapped on a hamster wheel in a rat race, and the only way out is if you're strong enough to break free. The structure of these systems is deceptively simple: provide just enough to keep people afloat, enough to prevent them from revolting but not enough to spark a widespread awakening of consciousness. This has conditioned us to live within the ordinary, to dream within the linear, and to accept only a fraction of what is truly possible. We've been taught to believe in limitations, not the vast, extraordinary potential of abundance.

As I write, I glance up at Mother Earth and see her abundant life force effortlessly thriving in her natural state. Yet I wonder how we've allowed artificial restrictions to limit our possibilities simply because someone somewhere said so. When I look again, I'm reminded of the opposite truth, the truth that Nature shows us every single day. No disaster, no matter how severe, can stop her from showing up tomorrow or the day after or for years to come. Even as she faces challenges like climate change and global warming, she still flourishes abundantly. Meanwhile, we let false narratives and limited thinking take centre stage in a life that we only get one chance to live.

From the moment of our conception, we are born as abundant beings. We are more than just our bodies; deep within us, emanating from our hearts, we are infinite potential, prodigies who have taken on the limitations humanity has imposed, leading us away from our natural states of abundant consciousness.

According to Bruce H. Lipton PhD[3], an internationally recognised leader in bridging science and spirit, stem cell biologist, our bodies house around 50 trillion cells, each containing 0.07 volts of energy. This means we carry 3.5 trillion volts of potential energy that we can harness and direct. Our electrically and magnetically charged cells create an invisible, doughnut-shaped electromagnetic field around us. If we could see it, we'd have a much clearer understanding of life's essence.

Your thoughts are the electrical charges in this field, while your emotions are the magnetic charges. This field originates from your heart centre and extends infinitely beyond your body. What you think and feel influences every cell in your being. Your thoughts send out signals, and the feelings you generate act as magnets, drawing events and experiences to you. The magnetic power of your feelings is far stronger than the electrical energy of your thoughts because your heart is 5,000 times more magnetically powerful than your brain. This is how your energy shapes the physical world around you.

---

3   Bruce H. Lipton, PhD is an internationally recognized leader in bridging science and spirit. Stem cell biologist, bestselling author of The Biology of Belief. https://www.brucelipton.com/what-are-the-volts-electricity-your-human-body/

Your thoughts and feelings directly shape the strength of your electromagnetic field within the metaphysical web. An abundant mindset expands your field infinitely, drawing an abundant array of possibilities into your life. A limited mindset, however, contracts your field to arm's length, leaving you with only the same possibilities you've already experienced. The electromagnetic field doesn't care about anything except your thoughts and feelings.

You have the power to redirect and reshape your life simply by adjusting your thought patterns and emotions. All that's required is for you to stop holding yourself back and start moving forward.

This is what it means to be the creator of your own reality.

As soon as you place limitations on yourself from within, you redefine abundance as a limited resource, closing the door to endless possibilities.

One of the most powerful yet underrated aspects of abundance is understanding it as something infinite, an energy that grows stronger when shared. Abundance expands when you pass it on, creating a cycle that makes you feel even more fulfilled than keeping it all for yourself. Infinite abundance means offering it not only to your friends but to your so-called 'enemies' as well. Every time you restrict abundance for someone else, you also limit it for yourself. True abundance is infinite because there is more than enough to go around for everyone. It's infinite because new resources are discovered every second, opening up even more possibilities. It's infinite in the way that you'll never have to clip coupons or hunt for discounts again. It's infinite because when you pay your bills, you'll be grateful that you get to do it.

Society has taught us to believe that life's force doesn't want us to experience infinite abundance because that would somehow be 'ungodly'. We are conditioned to be thankful for the smallest, modest things we have, as if abundance is a privilege we don't deserve.

We live in the fastest-paced, most prosperous capitalist society ever known. Millions, billions and even trillions of dollars circulate around us every moment, yet we live in our own little bubbles, blind to the vast wealth of possibilities. Meanwhile, we hold tight to the belief that money doesn't grow on trees, and we wonder why our lives seem limited in the same way. If you always settle for the cheapest or most mundane options, that is the energy you'll attract back into your life. Every cell of restriction within you will send a signal out to the universe that mirrors that limitation. It would be counterproductive and rude for your electromagnetic field to ignore your internal signals.

Mastering abundance means examining and understanding what blocks you from it. What thoughts and feelings do you hold that resist the flow of abundance? To truly embody infinity, you must confront how you feel about abundance itself and about others' abundance as well. If you feel envy or greed when others experience success, it's a sign that you need to do some inner work. Abundance doesn't recognise envy or greed. It thrives in an environment of generosity and openness. If these feelings arise when thinking of someone else's abundance, it's time to dig deeper.

As long as you hold on to beliefs like 'I must save for a rainy day,' it will inevitably rain on you. As long as you think 'It's too good to be true,' it will be. As long as you hoard abundance from others, you're blocking it from flowing freely into your life.

To live outside the confines of the 'matrix', to break free from limiting societal constructs, you must reconnect with your natural life force of limitless abundance. By emitting an expanding electromagnetic field that believes, *feels*, and radiates 'I can' and 'I will', you'll attract everything you need.

CHAPTER 5

Mirror, Mirror, On The Wall

"Life shrinks or expands in proportion to one's courage."

Anaïs Nin

The *Mirror Principle* is more than just a philosophy: it is a deep, life-changing truth. It holds the power to transform your life in ways you never thought possible, not by changing the world outside but by unlocking the potential within you. It's about tapping in, not tapping out. It is the key to understanding that everything you experience is a reflection of who you are on the inside. And when you truly grasp this, you will see that everything you've ever wanted, everything you've ever dreamed of, is already within your reach.

At its core, the Mirror Principle is this simple truth: *you must first become what you seek* within yourself before it can manifest in your life. Think of it like a mirror: when you stand before it and smile, the reflection automatically smiles back. You would never try to force the reflection to smile if your own face was scowling. The reflection simply cannot smile unless you do it first. The same law applies to every aspect of your life.

Some of you have been trying to tap in, but it's not the tap that leads to success. It's the tap that fuels your defeat. Many of us have tried to give up, not in the 'I surrender all' kind of way, but in the quiet, broken surrender that says, 'I'm done. I'm done loving fully. It's too painful. It leaves me too exposed.'

That's the tap that limitation relishes in. It doesn't want you to fight. It doesn't want you to press forward. It wants you to believe that retreat is easier, that pulling back is safer. But here's the truth: when you give up your freedom for the false comfort of old sequences, you may find a moment of relief, but you'll only sink deeper into a heavier kind of bondage. That's the lie it sells.

Self-pity has never led to progress; it never will. When you let it consume you, it doesn't lighten your load; it weighs you down even more. It keeps you anchored in your pain, so don't tap out; tap in. Tap into the fight. Tap into the strength you didn't know you had. Tap into the faith that refuses to quit even when the road is too hard and the journey too long.

When you tap out, you're only trading one prison for another, but when you tap in, you unlock the power to break free.

If you don't change within, nothing will change in your world. Life is not a random sequence of events; it is an exact reflection of your internal world, your beliefs, your feelings, your expectations. When life hands you challenges, *it is not life that is the problem,* it is you staring into the mirror of your own thoughts and feelings. When you begin to understand the Mirror Principle, you will come to realise that life does not give you lemons — you are the one handing them to yourself. Once you understand that, you will no longer feel like a victim of life; you will become the creator of it. You will realise that you have the power to change everything.

The reality you experience is nothing more than a mirror showing you the reflection of your *self-concept,* the relationship you have with yourself and your relationship with the world. Every situation, every event, every person you meet is a mirror that reflects your inner state. *The mirror will confirm* what you believe to be true about yourself and the world.

Take money, for example. If you believe that wealth is hard to come by, the mirror of reality will reflect that belief by presenting you with obstacles, struggles and hardships on the path to financial success. You will see the difficulties, the frustrations and the impossibilities. The mirror *must* reflect your inner conviction. Otherwise, it would defy the very laws of Nature.

And this is the beauty of it: You have the power to change the reflection. You don't need to struggle against the world outside you. You need to change the world inside you. The moment you shift your beliefs and your energy, the mirror of life will shift with you, and you'll suddenly see new possibilities, new opportunities, new pathways that were always there, just waiting for you to recognise them.

The Mirror Principle is the most powerful tool for self-mastery, for manifesting your deepest desires and for conquering challenges that seem insurmountable. When you understand that everything you see around you is simply a reflection of your internal state, you can begin to reshape your reality, one thought, one belief, one shift in perception at a time.

To live according to the Mirror Principle is to take full responsibility for your life and know, deep in your heart, that you are the creator of your experience. The more you embrace this truth, the more you realise that the life you desire has always been within you. All you need to do is change the way you see yourself and the world, and the mirror will do the rest.

Here are the principles:

1. **The mirror of reality is an unbreakable reflection of who you are and how you perceive the world.** Every thought, every belief and every emotion you hold about yourself and the world around you sends a powerful signal into the electromagnetic field, commanding it to bring forth more evidence to support your inner

reality. This is not a theory; this is the unshakable law of the universe. The mirror can only reflect what you think, what you feel and what you *believe* to be true. It doesn't bend, it doesn't compromise, it simply reflects. And it does so with a 100% success rate each and every time. There is no room for exceptions. The reality you experience is a mirror of the beliefs and thoughts you hold deep inside you.

2. **Reality itself does not exist until *you* observe it.** Supported by the ground-breaking discoveries of quantum physics, specifically the double-slit experiment, we understand that energy only collapses into physical form when observed by a conscious being. In other words, the universe itself waits for your perception to define it. Everything you see with your eyes, touch with your hands or hear with your ears is not solid; it is simply energy vibrating at frequencies slow enough for you to perceive as 'matter'. In fact, if you were to break down anything physical, you would find that it is 99.999% energy and only 0.00001% is matter.

3. **Energy creates matter.** This is the heart of creation. Einstein's equation, $E=mc^2$, revealed that energy and matter are not separate but are two sides of the same

coin. You are the observer, the creator and the shaper of your reality.

4. **Matter cannot change matter.** Society teaches us to manipulate the world outside us, to change people, to control situations to get what we want, but creation is not found in manipulating the external world; it is found in focusing your mind and your feelings on what you want. You are not a passive observer in this world; you are the architect of it.

5. **The reflection we see in the physical world is not instantaneous — it is a delayed manifestation of our inner world.** When we close our eyes, we can instantly visualise anything we desire, yet in the third dimension, the process is slower. Thoughts, beliefs, and desires don't immediately materialise because matter itself is dense, slow and bound by the laws of Nature. The chemistry of life doesn't allow for instant creation. It takes time for the energy to shift into physical form. Your present reality is simply the residue of your past thoughts, beliefs and emotions *burning off* in real-time. What you see now is the result of what you've previously created with your mind. The physical world you experience today is the harvest of yesterday's thoughts. This is why the world around you may not instantly reflect your desires, *but it will* in due time.

6. **You must hold unwavering faith in your beliefs until they fully take form in your physical reality.** This is where the true test of creation lies. When nothing changes right away, the temptation to lose faith can be overwhelming. You might question whether it's possible at all, and this doubt can create a downward spiral of negativity, but the key to change is this: *Do not allow your thoughts to return to lack or disbelief* when the world doesn't immediately reflect your desires. If you do, you'll only reinforce the very thing you are trying to escape: lack, struggle and scarcity. You must stand firm in your belief, unwavering in your commitment to the vision you are creating. The journey of creation is not linear. It will have its highs and lows, its moments of doubt and its periods of waiting, but through it all, you must remain steadfast, *devoted to the end result* regardless of what you see in front of you. Your belief, your commitment and your vision must be so unshakable that they *compel* reality to shift in alignment with you. **The creation process is a journey, not an event.** It's the commitment to your vision that makes it inevitable.

7. **The mirror of reality does not simply reflect the surface of your thoughts—it reflects their pure, unfiltered energy.** The universe does not care about the details of your thoughts; it only reflects the core vibration of what you believe. If you harbour resentment

towards paying bills, the mirror will reflect *more* bills back to you to reinforce that resentment. If you despise your job, the mirror will show you endless experiences that validate your hatred. If you believe relationships are hard, the world will deliver you partners and situations that prove just how difficult love can be. The more you focus on what you don't want, the more the Law of Nature will deliver exactly that. The universe is not biased. It only knows how to confirm what you believe, to validate your thoughts and emotions, whether positive or negative. It is a law as consistent as gravity.

When you look at your present reality—the nine-to-five job you don't want or the crushing weight of bills that exceed your income—don't allow this to define who you are. Most people only see their physical reality and believe that is all there is, trapping them in a repetitive loop bound by the illusion that seeing is believing. This belief keeps them stuck in a life of limitation, entirely disconnected from the deeper laws of life. So many of us remain trapped in this cycle, drifting through an entire life, wondering why we can't break free. If you want to become a true creator in your life, you must reverse the process. This philosophy demands that we stop seeking evidence in our external reality and instead turn inward. Don't look for proof in the mirror of your current reality; look for it in the power of your thoughts.

Take a moment to really pause and reflect on your life in this very moment. What do you see? Is it filled with love, or does it feel cold and disconnected? Is it messy and complicated, or does it flow with ease? Is it okay—quietly stable—or does it feel lonely and distant? **Is this the life you imagined?**

Without your thoughts, without your sense of self, there would be no reality to experience. Your consciousness is the lens through which everything is created. Your life isn't just happening to you; it's unfolding through you. If your heart aches for something more, know that you have the power to transform your inner landscape, and the world will follow.

At first, it may be hard to believe in the extraordinary. Your heart might resist, weighed down by doubts and fears. It can feel too far out of reach, too far from what you've known. But instead of pushing yourself to believe when you're not ready, meet yourself with kindness and grace. Replace the negativity with something softer: neutrality. Start with a simple thought like, 'What if everything is actually going to be okay?' It's not about forcing yourself to feel hopeful when it feels impossible; it's about opening a tiny space of trust.

Neutrality is the gentle bridge leading you out of the darkness. It's the quiet space between where you are and where you want to be. Every moment you allow yourself to shift from fear to neutrality, you move closer to your light and farther away from the weight of your worries. In that space, you give yourself permission to believe that something better is possible. And with each step, you bring yourself closer to the extraordinary life that's been waiting for you.

Once this way of thinking becomes your new truth, you will begin to notice signs that your manifestation is drawing near. You'll *see the birds before the land*. Now, you might not literally see birds flying overhead, but you'll start to notice the little synchronicities, the small, seemingly insignificant moments that feel like the universe is winking at you, saying, 'It's on its way.'

'Birds before the land' is a beautiful metaphor, the idea that birds never stray far from land, and so, when you see them, you know that land is near. It's the same with your dreams. As you begin to notice the signs, trust that your manifestation is getting closer, that it's just over the horizon. Your vision, your desires — they are not far away. The birds are the whispers of your future, and soon, you will see the land. And when you do, you'll know that you've arrived.

CHAPTER 6

The Crossroads of Possibility: Choice

"To live a creative life, we must lose our fear of being wrong."

Joseph Chilton Pearce

You choose what you do not change. Every moment is an encouragement to reshape your reality. You don't have to wait for a sign or a perfect moment. You can decide right now to pivot, to start over, to rewrite the script of your life. This is your moment to clear the debris of the past, to plant the seeds for a future that will light you up.

Choice is the pulse of your existence. It isn't reserved for the fortunate or the chosen few; it's woven into the fabric of every human being. The power to choose — to change, to release, to grow — is within you at all times. In every second, you can decide to let go of the weight of your past and rise into the person you're becoming. You can choose to heal, to forgive, to free yourself from whatever has been holding you captive, or you can choose to stay trapped in old patterns, in lingering pain. The decision is yours. Each thought you entertain, each feeling you embrace, is a call to reclaim your power. You are the source of your own energy, and you can direct it with intention.

Your power isn't outside of you. It flows through you, unshakable and eternal. Do not allow the false stories of the ego or the limiting beliefs it whispers to diminish your light.

If you long for freedom, joy and peace, choose them. Choose to embody them right now in this very moment.

Don't wait for the stars to align or for things to fall into place. Choose to feel free, to feel joy, to feel at peace *now*. If you crave love, abundance and prosperity, become the centre of that love, abundance and prosperity. Draw those blessings towards you by choosing to believe in your own worthiness, by choosing to see the beauty of what's already here.

You can always choose to see the fullness in your life, the possibilities instead of the limitations. It's your choice whether you face the world with fear or with an open heart, whether you choose to see the best in others or project your doubts onto them. You have the power to decide that today is a day of opportunity, a day of expansion, a day where you step into a different life.

Your life is unfolding in direct response to the choices you make today. Each decision, no matter how small, is a brushstroke on the canvas of your future. You are the author of your story, the creator of your experience, and you hold the pen in your hand, **so choose boldly.** Choose from a place of deep knowing. Choose with the certainty that the world is ready for you to step into your greatness.

YOU CAN

A Series

The *You Can Series* is not just a collection of ideas—it is a clarion call to awaken your infinite potential. This is not about choosing a different path; it's about choosing to live the life you were always meant to live, a life that pulses with passion, purpose and an unwavering belief that you deserve to be extraordinary. This is your invitation to stop *existing* and start *living*, to create with intention and to choose powerfully every single day.

Abundance is not a gift handed out to a select few; it is your divine birthright. It is not something reserved for those lucky enough to 'get chosen' by the universe. It is something you actively *choose*, *claim* and *embody*. Abundance is the natural state of being, and it all begins with the choice you make to step into it. You don't need to wait for a sign. You don't need permission from anyone. Right now, you only need to decide to become a person who is worthy of everything you desire.

No one else can walk this path for you. You must break free from the conditioning that has kept you small; the programming passed down from generation to generation, the beliefs that have limited your possibilities, the fears that have locked you into a life of mediocrity. When you shed these illusions, you will open the door to a universe of limitless potential, a universe that is waiting for you to step into it. Yes, even if no one around you has ever walked this path. Yes, even if they think you're crazy or if they don't understand. This journey isn't for them — it's for you. You are the one who will break the cycle, who will recalibrate your life and the lives of those who come after you. You are here for something greater than what you've been taught to settle for.

This series will show you exactly how to travel through the limiting walls of your conditioned beliefs and step into your fullest potential. It is not just a book — it is a profound shift in how you see yourself and the world around you. It will teach you how to recalibrate your consciousness, to stop holding yourself back and start living the life of your dreams, starting today. This is where you stop waiting for the perfect moment and start *creating* it.

Here, you will learn to choose the frequency of your highest self, the version of you who knows no limits, who understands that abundance is not a possibility but an inevitability. You will tap into a vibration that doesn't ask for permission, a vibration that *commands* the universe to meet you at your highest potential. You don't need any external validation. All you need is your mind, your soul and your willingness to choose greatness.

If you're not where you want to be, it's because you haven't made the choice with the full power and clarity it requires.

This is your call to step into a higher level of consciousness, where you no longer wait for abundance to show up. You create it moment by moment, breath by breath. Every thought, every belief, every action is a conscious act of co-creation. Abundance doesn't just happen; it's a choice, and that choice is yours to make.

This series will illuminate and show you your *minimum standards*, the unconscious expectations you've set for yourself. Abundant people operate from a different level. If you don't yet know what your minimum standard is, just take a look at your life right now. What do you settle for? What do you accept as 'good enough'? It's time to raise the bar. This is your permission slip to demand more for yourself, to refuse to settle for anything less than the highest vision you can imagine. It's time to stop being grateful for what you have and start being grateful for what you *will* have because you know you were born for magnificence.

If something within you is calling, if there is a dream burning in your heart, it's already happening in your future. That fire is your soul speaking to you, showing you what's possible. Mastery comes when you learn how to alchemise your thoughts, your feelings and your energy to create the reality you desire. When you shift your inner world, you bend time and space itself, pulling your future into the present.

It's time to listen to your soul, not just once a year when you check in on your vision board but every single moment. The future you want is already in your energy. It's already inside you. The only thing left is for you to embody it fully and unapologetically.

There is not a single person living in true abundance who doesn't know exactly how it arrived in their life. They have mastered the art of choice, the art of knowing that abundance is not an accident but a direct result of their unwavering faith and intention. The *You Can Series* will take you to the point where you no longer need to repeat affirmations because abundance won't just be something you 'believe' in — it will become who you are. Just like you don't need to remind yourself the sky is blue, you won't need to remind yourself that abundance is your natural state. It will be as unquestionable and as constant as the air you breathe.

If you have a vision that has yet to materialise, it's because there are cracks in the foundation of your self-worth. I am here to help you fill those cracks, to heal the wounds that have kept you from stepping into your power. Together, we will rebuild the relationship you have with yourself so you can manifest everything your heart desires.

This series will empower you to recognise the unconscious patterns, beliefs and frequencies that have held you hostage.

You are a one-in-eight-billion miracle. There is no one else like you, and no one else can leave the imprint on the world that you are meant to leave. You have been given a unique fingerprint, a soul print that no one else in the history of the world has. The question is, will you claim it?

At the end of each chapter, you will find integration questions designed to ignite a deep relationship with yourself. This is the moment when you stop pretending to be someone you're not and start embodying the person you were always meant to become. These questions are not just prompts — they are your keys to awakening, to living a life where you are free to be your authentic self and create everything you've ever desired.

If you want to see what abundance can really do in your life, then turn the page. The journey starts now.

You Can Alchemise Your Inner Culture

"Believe you can, and you're halfway there."

Theodore Roosevelt

There is nothing in this world that doesn't start with *you*. And so, I will always begin with *you*, just as I had to begin with myself.

It may seem simple, even obvious, if I asked you, 'Do you know who you are?' You'd probably answer without hesitation, 'Of course, I do,' but the truth is, you may not know yourself as deeply as you think. Or perhaps how much you're blind to.

Seven years ago, I was *so sure* I knew exactly who I was. I thought I had it all figured out, but looking back, I realise I couldn't have been further from the truth. And you know what? That's okay because if you find that you've been wrong about yourself, it's not a failure — it's the first step toward *real* growth. And it only gets better from here.

If you haven't done the deep, quiet work of understanding your true essence, you won't know how to truly evolve. Without this clarity, it's impossible to build a life with a lasting purpose. The honest, unflinching recognition of who you really are is the foundation for everything that comes next.

Without it, you're trying to build a house without a solid foundation. No matter how much you try, without clear self-awareness, you'll never create a mission, a vision, or a lasting impact. Instead, you'll find your life filled with confusion and distractions. Without that deep understanding of yourself, you'll create nothing but clutter.

So, this journey begins with you. Not the version of you that you show the world but the real you, the one waiting for you to *see* them, to *know* them. When you do, everything else in your life will begin to fall into place.

I realised something deep within me: we pour so much of our energy into the rat race, chasing the approval and success others set for us, yet we neglect the most important thing of all: *ourselves*. At work, we jump, we leap, we run, constantly seeking feedback, trying to climb higher, to prove our worth, but when it comes to our own lives, we shy away from the chance to look inward, to ask the hard questions, to give ourselves the honest feedback we need to grow.

The first step in awakening is simply this: knowing that awareness *is* sleeping inside you, and the moment you admit that to yourself, it will stir. It will begin to awaken, to shift something inside you. But if you believe that ignorance is peace, that what you don't know won't hurt you, then this book, this journey, isn't for you. Close it now and pass it on.

If you're still here, if you're still reading, then I want you to hear this: *Consciousness is healing.* It's the very key to freeing yourself.

To grow, to heal, to reclaim who you truly are, you must learn to sit with yourself, to *feel* your own reflections, and, yes, to welcome both assessment and feedback from within. Your self-concept, the way you see and understand yourself, is the foundation of everything: your joy, your peace, your sense of purpose. It's the one place where you have full control over how much love and care you choose to pour in. And when you feel doubt or frustration creeping in, when you notice your energy leaving you to seek validation elsewhere, *that's your sign that* the soil of your heart needs attention. It's thirsty. It needs nurturing. Your self-concept is the very root of everything you will ever need.

So, water it, care for it and watch how everything in your life starts to flourish from within.

It is *crucial*—no, it is life-changing—that as we passionately pursue the life we envision, we learn to *unravel* our sense of self-worth from the things we desire. It's far too easy for our worth to become entangled with our dreams, our goals, our endless lists of manifestations. We believe that once we finally achieve this *one thing*—this elusive desire—we'll finally feel whole, finally be seen as beautiful, courageous, worthy. We convince ourselves that this external thing, this outcome, is the key to unlocking our value, but this is where we're misled. Our desires are *rooted* in ego. They are born from the belief that we are incomplete, that something outside of us is needed to make us feel *enough*.

As humans, we have this tendency to lose ourselves in our desires. We obsess, we chase, and we make these things the focal point of our happiness, of our worth, of our entire existence. We become so fixated on them that we lose sight of the most powerful truth of all: **You are already whole.** You are already enough. Right now. In this moment. A solid self-concept is the realisation that your worth is *unshakeable*, even without those things you crave. It's not about repeating mantras or chasing signs that your desires are just around the corner. It's about *feeling* your wholeness, your *worthiness* deep within. It's about *owning* the truth that you are not defined by what you achieve, what you acquire or how others see you.

The truth is this: you don't need anything outside of yourself to validate your worth. No object, no person, no success, no failure should alter how you truly feel about who you are. You are not defined by what you do, what you have or what you've yet to manifest. Your worth is intrinsic, *unbreakable* and *eternal.* And when you finally stand in full recognition of this, when you feel it in your body and your soul, that's when everything you've ever desired will come into alignment, not because you *need* it but because you are already complete.

Before we begin, let me make you one promise: If you uncover the *truth* of who you are — if you truly know yourself — you will have the power to create worlds, move mountains and shatter every limitation in your path. Nothing will ever feel impossible again. So, let's dive in.

Self-concept (your state of being): It's everything you think, believe and feel about yourself, both consciously and subconsciously. It's your identity, your foundation, and it shapes every single thing in your life.

Your current self-concept is a product of the past: the same thoughts, feelings, behaviours and habits. It's a bank of all the accumulated information, experiences and memories of everything up to this point. Your level of mind reaps the same rewards over and over again, meaning your level of mind has remained the same. You are living in a time that does not exist anymore, and you wonder why change doesn't happen, *right?*

You can then undeniably say the *only* places where the past exists are your mind and your body.

Your state of being is shaped by how you think and feel. If you keep thinking the same thoughts and feeling the same emotions, you're living in the past. These are the thoughts and feelings you've already experienced over and over. Anything you know—whether it's a thought, a feeling or an action—is a product of what's already happened. If you can predict how an experience will make you feel, or what thoughts will come up in a situation, you're living as a by-product of yesterday. As long as your self-concept stays the same, you'll keep reaping the same results because the mind shapes reality. By staying in familiar patterns, you keep a uniform mind, and with it, the same odds, the same struggles, the same Wednesdays. Now, think about the thoughts you've had about yourself today: Are they new, or are they just echoes of yesterday?

When we repeatedly think, feel, behave and act the same way, our brains create automatic neurological programs that make it easier to stay trapped in those patterns. Emotions are the body's language, and when we continually feel the same emotions, we condition our bodies to live in the past. Over time, our bodies begin to function on autopilot, doing things without conscious thought, allowing our physical state to become a mirror of our minds. But when you decide to break free, when you start thinking and feeling in new ways, when you choose to play in the soil of *infinite possibility*, you step into the unknown. Your 'What if this happens?' thoughts are the seeds of your transformation.

When you think a thought, neurons fire in your brain sending electrical signals that chemically react to create a feeling, an emotion, which, in turn, generates magnetic charges. This dynamic fusion of thoughts and feelings create an electromagnetic field around your body, a field that matches the frequency of your self-concept. At the beginning of the book, when I said that you needed to start living from a place of energy, I wasn't speaking metaphorically. Once you understand the true nature of reality, you'll never see life the same way again, but if you remain trapped in the same self-concept, you'll keep transmitting the same electromagnetic field day after day, stuck in the same limited cycle of ordinary possibility. If you want to break free, if you want something new to unfold in your life, it starts by changing the very energy you project through your thoughts and emotions.

I came across something recently that deeply resonated with everything we've been talking about. It went something like this: A crab must undergo a process called moulting in order to grow. As it gets bigger, its hard shell becomes too tight, too suffocating, causing the crab pain and discomfort. In order to grow, it must shed its old shell and form a new, larger one, but here's the catch: This process is risky. It leaves the crab vulnerable, exposed to danger because it has no protection in the interim. Yet this step—this painful, dangerous shedding—is absolutely necessary for growth.

Epigenetics reveals a powerful truth: it's not your genes that create disease but the environment that programs them. And that environment is *your emotions*. Your emotions shape the environment in which your body exists. When you repeatedly feel the same way, your genes continue to receive the same signals. And because your body is conditioned to the known, to safety, to the comfort of what's familiar, it becomes *harder* to break free, to change, to evolve.

This is why self-analysis is absolutely crucial. It's not just about influencing matter with your mind; it's about preparing your body to experience the unknown, to step beyond the limits of what you've always known. So, to those who say that feelings don't matter, *they do*. To those who tell you to stop being emotional, *don't you dare*. Your emotions are the magnetic charge that creates worlds. Don't waste them. Harness them. Use them to *transform* your reality.

SENSES

The more I journeyed through life, the more I discovered the truth. I came to realise that the physical world we experience wouldn't even exist without our senses. It's through our senses that we detect, assess and interpret the material world. Without sight, smell, sound, taste or touch, I would never know the warmth of a friend's hug, the sweetness of a strawberry or the hum of a car engine. In fact, I wouldn't know so many of the things I hold dear in this world.

But here's the thing: the majority of people are conditioned to focus solely on what is tangible, on the material, that they live in a state of limitation. Most believe that seeing is believing, that if you can't prove something with physical evidence, it's far-fetched, impossible.

This is the silent crisis, the deep-rooted trap. From a young age, we are taught to think within the narrow confines of a limited mind, pushed further away from the true, boundless mechanics of Nature. With such finite minds, we've come to believe that reality is defined only by what we can see, hear, touch or measure. We've been trained only to value what's visible, only what's already been experienced, but when you limit yourself to the world of the senses, when you define your reality and your potential based on what you've already seen, what you've already known, you will be forever cut off from a life of infinite possibility.

Stay with me.

By defining your life purely in terms of matter, you chain yourself to a narrow, predictable reality, one where only a few things can ever truly happen for you. If this is how you live, then you're a materialist, someone who believes, feels and predicts everything based on what the physical world shows them. If you wait to be employed to feel rich or depend on a relationship to feel worthy, you're a materialist because you rely on external circumstances to determine how you feel. If you live your life governed by the weight of your 'terrible upbringing', you're not only a materialist, but you're someone still trapped in the past, still living at the age of your trauma. If you care more about how you're perceived than who you truly are, you're channelling your energy outward into things that don't define your essence. And if you believe history is doomed to repeat itself, guess what? You're still a materialist.

The cold, hard truth is this: Matter is limiting, predictable and *safe*. It keeps you locked in the same loop, only experiencing what you already know.

If you can sense something, you can confirm that it's real, tangible and separate from you, but here's the thing: *Nothing is physically attached to your body.* Your car, this book, your phone, even your mother—they're not part of you. You look around and see separation everywhere: people, objects, experiences, all standing apart from you, and in doing so, you reinforce a life of survival, not creation. Separation breeds lack—it keeps you small, distant and disconnected—but oneness? Oneness brings abundance. It opens the door to a world where you are the creator, not a passive observer. The material world only reinforces the illusion of separation, and by clinging to it, you remain bound to the past, to everything you've already experienced.

So, what's the solution? You must live beyond your senses. You must invest your focus in your inner world, making it more real than the material world you interact with every day. If the material world is limited, the immaterial world is limitless. This is the Law of Polarity. To create greater opportunities and possibilities, you must live immaterially. Overcoming any obstacle allows you to reclaim your energy. When your energy, once spent on matter, is brought back to you, it can be used to create anything as extraordinary as you wish.

Re-identifying yourself is crucial. If you still define yourself by your trauma from 2008 or the person you were in 2012, you will continue to live in that version of yourself, even if it's 2026. Your identity starts to shift when you check in with yourself. The more flexible you become, the more you can shape a new identity. This happens when you force your brain to envision a new narrative, a new belief, a new possibility, a miracle, as we call it. If you identify with your body, your home or your job, you are restricting yourself to a limited reality. When you align with matter, you lose your connection to the infinite. To create a new life, a new future, you cannot let your identity be defined by the past or the material world in front of you.

When you see others wishing on stars, reaching for the impossible, and you wonder — *what do they know that I don't?* — they're seeing life through a lens of energy, not matter. Fixating on the material world is what keeps you stuck in places you don't want to be, so don't blame the players; blame the game. You've become a materialist, not because you desire material things but because you've been led to believe that manipulating the physical world is the only way to create a life that works for you.

For example, let's consider quantum entanglement. This mind-boggling phenomenon shows us how two subatomic particles can be deeply connected, even if they're separated by billions of light years. Despite their distance, a change in one particle instantly affects the other. They move in unison, mimicking each other's behaviour, no matter the space between them. Even though they're not physically connected, they share information across vast distances in the blink of an eye. This proves that everything around you operates in this same interconnected way. Nothing is truly separate. We are all linked as one on this planet. You are in a constant, energetic relationship with everyone and everything. When you elevate your own energy—when you grow happier, healthier—the entire world around you will shift and align, just like those particles.

So, if your reality feels stuck, if nothing seems to change, perhaps it's time to ask yourself whether you're still living as a materialist. If you continue creating from the same frequency, from the same energy that matches the current state of your life, nothing new will emerge. You must rise above matter. You must feel and believe greater than what you see in front of you, or you'll never create space for the infinite possibilities waiting just beyond the horizon.

Instead of anchoring your future to past experiences, you must place every ounce of your faith in the *'even if'*. Even if I've experienced XYZ, even if my past has been full of setbacks, an unknown possibility far greater than anything I've ever imagined is waiting for me. The more you invest in the realm of the unknown—where the boundaries of your current life no longer apply—the more new and unexplored circumstances will emerge, birthing a new reality. But if you continue to focus on the material, you suffocate possibility.

We're here to experience life beyond our five senses. There are possibilities so vast, so extraordinary that you wouldn't even know to ask for them because you've been conditioned to believe in the finite, in the material world. You will only discover how magnificent life can truly be once you release the grip on your past investments that have borne no fruit. You must out-sense, out-dream, out-think, out-know and out-predict yourself. Maybe you've been standing under an umbrella for too long, hiding from the rain, but maybe, just maybe, it's time to step out into the storm and let it show you what's possible. Live beyond your senses, and witness how far you can go.

THE PAST

We often forget that we have the power to reinvent ourselves at any moment. The moment you step into a new version of yourself with a redefined self-concept, the past will lose its grip on you because you are no longer that person. You've transcended it.

Identifying your belief systems is the first step towards true freedom. By examining your beliefs, you can spot those that no longer align with your truth. It's like being in a store and trying on a pair of shoes that don't fit—you simply take them off and move on. The same goes for your beliefs. If they no longer resonate with who you are, let them go. When you're unconscious of a belief it controls you, but once you bring it into awareness, it can no longer have power over you. You can choose not to let it define your reality.

When I speak of integrating a new self-concept, I mean becoming a completely new person. If you truly understand that you're crafting a new identity, you must also embrace a different past. If we only exist in the present moment, then the past is nothing more than a story we tell ourselves about what happened based on the present. From this moment forward, you can choose to define your past as it's always been, or you can redefine it according to what you wish it had been. If you keep it tied to the old story, you'll remain tethered to the same thoughts and emotions, but if you rewrite your past to fit the person you are becoming, you'll create space for progressive self-continuity and open the door to a new future. When you become a new person, your past will transform with you.

Your self-concept is the ultimate foundation for progress, peace and purpose. When you dedicate yourself to the things no one can ever take from you—your inner strength, your beliefs, your vision—you become unstoppable. It's time to release the weight of the past and let bygones truly be bygones so you can rise into a life of unshakable greatness.

SUMMARY

When things aren't going your way, it's time to ask yourself: *What do I believe about myself that's holding me back from experiencing the reality I desire?* By consciously choosing to affirm your worthiness, your desirability and your irreplaceability from within, you'll transform into a person who radiates confidence, someone who knows they are unconditionally loved, chosen and cherished. When you truly embody the belief that you are loved, worthy, rich and important, the opinions of Tom, Dick or Harry will no longer control your sense of self.

All those endless struggles, the long battles and short-lived efforts that never seem to work out—they're not random, suspicious or coincidences. They're signs that it's time to change your self-concept. Every experience you face is a reflection of who you are becoming. Nothing is happening to you by accident. It's all unfolding to help you evolve, to help you sprout into the next version of yourself.

How long will you mourn an old season, past relationships or long-lost glory? Stop idolising what's behind you and make space for the new things waiting to unfold. Look ahead to where you're being led and stop clinging to what's already gone. There is always a way forward. If you can't walk, crawl. If you can't shout, whisper. If you can't see, trust and believe.

INTEGRATION

1. **Reflect on three ways you've repeatedly failed to honour your self-worth.** The patterns you keep participating in are the roots of your deepest negative beliefs. It's vital to bring awareness to these wounds and allow yourself to grieve them because if ignored, they'll scar and become embedded in your identity. Now, take a moment to write three powerful ways in which you can begin to truly respect yourself, starting today.

2. **Explore the phrase, 'The reason I don't believe in myself is because' five times.** Each time, let it guide you to a deeper realisation. Then, rewrite each one as a powerful affirmation: why *you can* believe in yourself.

3. **List five areas where you currently hold pessimism.** What are the hidden payoffs in continuing to believe in these limiting thoughts? Dig deep to uncover why you're holding onto them and what's really keeping you resistant to change. What's the story you're telling yourself?

You Can Transcend The Victim

'The real mission you have in life is to make yourself happy, and in order to be happy, you have to look at what you believe, the way you judge yourself, the way you victimize yourself.'

Miguel Ruiz

In this episode, I show you yourself. I hold up a mirror, both brutally honest and deeply intimate. Before this journey even begins, you will confront every buried, raw and untamed part of you, every shadow, every wound both hidden and exposed, not just for what they are, but for where they will take you. You will stand face-to-face with your truth, *purging* what no longer serves you and claiming what is yours to keep. This is the crucible where you will transcend darkness into light and victimhood into unstoppable power.

We live in a world obsessed with fighting the inevitable. People do anything to slow the march of time. First, they deny it's happening, then they throw themselves into makeup, fitness and fashion, hoping to turn back the clock, but when that facade inevitably crumbles — and it always does — they're left confronting a truth they've been trying to outrun. Changing your face is now the norm, but changing your mind? That's where the real revolution happens, and it's the one they'll burn you for.

Transcending the victim is understanding that everything in your field of vision is a direct extension of your mind. If you could grasp that every single thing you experience in the external world is, in fact, a projection of *you*, then you would see there is no fancy house, no luxury car, no dream career. There is only *you* and *your mind*. Your thoughts, your beliefs, your vision. This means that your free will doesn't just manifest love, joy and connection — it also breeds competition, envy and fear.

When you realise everything is a reflection of your imagination, blame loses its power. There is no one and nothing to change but your mind. Once you realise this truth, you will stop seeking validation through external accomplishments. You'll understand that what truly matters isn't what you can show others but what you can create within yourself. If you know that everything you encounter is a product of your mind, there is no need for blame. There is no one or no thing outside of you that must change, only the inner beliefs and imagination you choose to cultivate.

Most people get trapped in this cycle because they believe the external world is the real one. When they say, 'Get back to reality,' they are unknowingly binding themselves to the very limitations they've accepted in their minds. In truth, reality isn't in the material world; it's in the mind. If you're stuck in a loop, it's because you've accepted a reality that isn't yours to begin with. The moment you realise that your external world is a reflection of your internal world, everything shifts. You no longer have to 'get back' to anything. You'll have the power to create an entirely new reality from within.

When you're asked who you want to be, nine times out of 10, your answer will be tied to some external title. If you say, 'I want to be happy,' let's be real—it won't have the same impact as saying, 'I want to be a millionaire.' The world values things that can be seen, touched and quantified, but here's the truth: everything you chase outside of yourself—money, fame, status, recognition—is nothing but a fleeting glimpse of happiness. Happiness based on the external is fragile, like building a mansion on quicksand. It can never be your foundation because it's rooted in illusion.

The moment you truly know who you are—not in fragments but in the fullness of your being—you'll stop questioning why things unfold the way they do. When you have a profound understanding of your essence, your power and your purpose, nothing feels random. You trust in the certainty that you can shape your reality because you know yourself so deeply you know exactly what needs to be altered to manifest the life you desire.

When you carry skepticism, distrust and weakness within yourself, you unknowingly embody a victim mindset. The truth is, when you don't trust your own strength, you don't trust that you hold the power to transform your life. Without that belief in yourself, you end up relying on the external world to shape your reality, to hand you the answers, to deliver the change you crave. When it doesn't show up the way you expect, you find yourself wallowing in a 'Poor me?' or 'Why me?' narrative.

If you believe others hold more power than you, they will. If you can't see the depth of your own worth and responsibility, you'll unconsciously hand it over to someone or something that seems to know better. But here's the real question: When will you take back that power? When will you stop letting the world dictate who you are and what you can create? The moment you fully accept that you are the creator of your own life—no excuses, no blaming—you'll step into your fullest potential.

An experiment was conducted with a group of women to see if people with facial disfigurements faced discrimination. They were shown scars on their faces and told they would be going to job interviews. However, before the women left the room, the researchers subtly removed the scars, and the women went into the interviews thinking they were still disfigured. When they returned, many reported feeling an increase in discrimination, and many even mentioned comments the interviewers had made that they felt referred to their scars.

Here's the key takeaway: the women's perception of themselves, not their actual appearance, created the experience of discrimination. It wasn't the scars on their faces that caused the bias; it was the belief that they were scarred. This experiment shows how our internal beliefs can shape how we experience the world. **When you believe something about yourself, you create an energy that the world mirrors back to you.** The women's sense of being 'flawed' made them see and feel discrimination, even when it wasn't there. This shows that the way we view ourselves becomes the lens through which we interact with everything around us.

A victim complex is something you cultivate for yourself through the stories you tell and the feelings you reinforce. Whether you wear it like a badge of honour or tragedy, it's crucial to build the courage to acknowledge that you've been the one victimising yourself. When you identify as being a victim of the world instead of being one with it, you limit your true potential. You restrict your ability to perform at your best, to rise to your true competencies and to fully experience life's opportunities.

When you define yourself as a victim, it becomes all too easy to see the world as a trap, a matrix that's been forced upon you. You will feel powerless, trapped in a cycle of circumstances beyond your control, but here's the truth: no one can impose anything on you unless you allow it. The moment you stop defining yourself as a victim, the victimhood dissolves. If you keep believing you're a victim, you'll continue to see proof of it everywhere, whether it's in your relationships, your career or the way life unfolds. Your mind will hunt for that narrative, and you'll find things that confirm it because you've conditioned yourself to believe it.

When you constantly search outside yourself for the reasons behind your pain and struggles, you rob yourself of the power to transform. You will stop looking inward for the keys to your freedom. The real work begins when you stop blaming the world and start facing the parts of yourself that need healing, nurturing and growth. Only then can you step into the full power of who you truly are. If you truly understand that everything around you exists because you created it, you'll stop victimising yourself. You'll begin to clean out your mind, clearing away the debris of old beliefs and limitations. Only when you let go of your victim mindset will you tap into the infinite power within you. As long as you refuse to believe that your thoughts and feelings shape your reality, you'll remain a victim, waiting for the world or others to change things for you.

Your life, your creation, is in your hands. Own it, or watch it slip away in the pursuit of others' approval.

The ego thrives on shifting all responsibility to the external world because it allows you to point fingers, deflect blame and avoid facing the truth of your own power, but the ego is not your enemy—it's a part of you, a fantastic tool for self-awareness. Instead of submitting to it, listen. The ego speaks the very truths you need to confront in order to grow. It will always highlight what needs to be alchemised within you. Its purpose isn't to keep you trapped but to help you recognise where you're holding yourself back. The key is not to fight the ego but to transcend its limitations and transform its influence into a catalyst for expansion, growth and conscious evolution.

Happiness is often tied to success and material possessions: cars, watches, diamonds, clothes. Many chase these, believing, 'If I have, then I am,' but when you step back, you'll see how empty this pursuit is. You can't use someone else's map to find your own path. True fulfilment comes from within, not from external validation.

If I took away everything external—money, possessions, achievements—would you still feel happy and fulfilled? Without the material world, what would you strive for?

If you find yourself trapped in a reality you despise, the only thing standing between you and the life you truly desire is the unconscious belief you're unknowingly holding onto.

You don't cling to anything unless you believe it serves you, no matter how destructive it is. So, if you continue choosing paths that disempower you, there's a hidden belief that's making them seem beneficial, even when they aren't. That belief is either chaining you to your past or propelling you towards your destiny. It's time to take back your power and recognise that nothing — *nothing* — outside of you can control your fate.

If you truly loved yourself, you would already be living the life you desire. If you took full responsibility for your choices, your circumstances would shift to reflect your power. If you trusted yourself completely, the life you want would unfold before you.

INTEGRATION

1. **Identify three situations in which you've seen yourself as a victim.** For each situation, reflect on the hidden benefits or payoffs that have kept you in this victim mindset. How has this belief served you, even if it may no longer be beneficial?

2. **List five people you've blamed during times of struggle.** After each name, write down a positive and empowering reason why you no longer need to blame them. Focus on the lessons you've learnt, how they've contributed to your growth, or how you can now take responsibility for your own actions and responses.

3. **Explore the statement: 'I cannot take accountability because...'** Now, counter each of your reasons with three compelling reasons why you *can* take full accountability. What would be possible if you embraced responsibility in every situation, regardless of external circumstances?

You Can Live By The Fifth

'The man who has no imagination has no wings.'

Muhammad Ali

Before diving deeper into this episode, it's essential to distinguish between the **Third Dimension (3D)** and the **Fifth Dimension (5D)**.

THE THIRD DIMENSION (3D)

The third dimension is the world we experience with our senses: past, present and future. It's the physical realm, governed by solid matter. In scientific terms, the 3D is a substance that retains its size and shape, where molecules don't move freely but only vibrate. This dimension is all about external matter; we give it power, and our lives revolve around moving and manipulating it to survive. In 3D, life is about effort, work and external achievements, often just enough to get by. The typical 3D existence is focused on 'working hard' for decades only to have a few years left to enjoy life (if health permits). This dimension is fixed and objective. Reality is created based on what you can touch, see and measure. It's a world of limitations, where time is linear and restricted by the physical. Life there feels predetermined; you're defined by your circumstances, and success often feels like something you're working towards but never fully grasp. It's a way of life based on doing, achieving and fulfilling external expectations. Reality in the 3D world is concrete, predictable and often devoid of true possibility beyond what is seen and known.

However...

THE FIFTH DIMENSION (5D)

The fifth dimension is subjective, unique to each of the 8 billion souls on Earth. It's an open realm, accessible at any point in your life because no one can ever stop you from thinking or feeling. In this space, everything in your reality is shaped by your thoughts and emotions. Everything that happens in your world occurs based on your personal truth, your consciousness and not anyone else's. This dimension is where your thoughts, feelings and energy directly influence the world around you. In the 5D, you create your reality through your frequency. Your attention, your focus and the energy you emit are what shape your experiences. What you think and feel attracts the circumstances, people and events that resonate with your inner state.

In this chapter and beyond, shifting from the third to the fifth dimension should become your new way of being. Choosing to live by the fifth dimension means transcending your environment and letting your mind lead the way. In the fifth dimension, energy is rerouted towards possibility, and the potential for transformation is limitless.

When you focus solely on the material world, you block the door to transformation. By fixating on your possessions, the people around you and everything external that defines you, you confine yourself to linear space: time and circumstance. But your mind has the power to transcend these limits. Through meditation, you can enter the quantum field, a realm beyond time and space made of invisible energy, frequencies and endless possibilities. This field is not accessed through your five senses but through your consciousness. To enter it, you must release your attachment to the physical dimension. To become pure consciousness, you must detach from everything in the material world. Only then can you tap into the infinite potential that exists beyond the physical, where all possibilities unfold not through effort but through alignment.

You might be curious how humanity came to understand the quantum universe, so let me share a brief story about quantum electrodynamics, one that won't take up too much of your time.

The Quantum Field Theory is regarded as one of the most accurate and powerful theories in modern physics. Dr Edgar Mitchell, former *Apollo* astronaut, refers to it as

'Nature's Mind'[4]. Stephen Hawking called it 'the Mind of God'[5], while most simply refer to it as 'the Field'. In 1980, David Bohm, called it 'the matrix'[6]. Scientists first discovered the quantum field when they studied the subatomic realm. They found that atoms consist of a nucleus surrounded by a vast field containing one or more electrons. This field is so vast compared to the electrons that it seemed like 99.999 % empty space, but this 'empty' space is far from void; it's alive with a pulsating essence of energetic frequencies.

In the quantum field, scientists observed that electrons behave in ways that defy conventional logic. One moment, they could be here, and the next, they could be somewhere entirely different—it's impossible to predict where or when they'll show up. Over time, they uncovered that electrons exist simultaneously in an infinite number of possibilities. Dr Joe Dispenza, author and researcher of epigenetics, quantum physics & neuroscience,[7] explains this phenomenon by stating that the quantum field is

4   Mitchell, E. D. (2000). Nature's mind: the quantum hologram. Journal of Computing Anticipatory Systems, 7, 295–312.
5   Stephen Hawking, A Brief History of Time (New York: Bantam Books, 1988), 174.
6   David Bohm, Wholeness and the Implicate Order (London: Routledge, 1980), 134.
7   https://drjoedispenza.com/dr-joes-blog/change-the-field-change-matter-part-ii

a realm of pure potential where the particles we observe in our reality are not fixed but exist in a state of infinite possibility until they are observed and collapse into a specific form. This insight reveals that reality is not as concrete as we once believed but is, instead, fluid, malleable and influenced by our conscious awareness.

From this, we can gather that particles of physical matter, such as electrons, do not exist in their fixed form until we direct our attention to them. The moment we withdraw our focus, they revert back into pure energy and possibility.

Now, you might wonder how this applies to you and how you can use this knowledge to transform your life.

When we stop giving our attention to the things we don't like—such as our pain, our lack, our health issues or our uninspiring routines—they, too, return to their original states of energy and potential. Just like the electrons that disappeared and reappeared in the quantum field when not observed, the things in your life can also transform. By simply shifting your focus, you can open up new experiences and possibilities. It's important to understand that just as we cannot predict where or when an electron will show up, we cannot impose a specific timeframe or location on our manifestations. You don't need to know the 'how' or the 'when'. What matters is that you hold a clear intention and maintain an aligned emotional state. This allows the quantum field to organise the details and place you in the ideal condition for your desires to come to fruition.

The fifth dimension empowers you to shape reality with the power of your mind beyond the labels of title, gender, race, age, material possessions and the weight of the past. The rigid constructs of the third dimension—those artificial boundaries and identities—obscure our true connection to the infinite. In survival mode, we constantly scan our external environments for threats, shifting our focus toward matter and away from energy. In this state, we become more anchored in the 3D physical world and less connected to the expansive 5D realm, where possibility and creation are limitless.

Operating solely from the 3D realm tightens your focus, shrinks your perception and chains you more to materialism. When your attention is fixated on manipulating matter with matter, you become locked in a cycle of limitation. If you're living in a state of lack but continue to affirm, 'I am abundant,' you won't see any true change. Affirmations alone aren't enough; true creation unfolds when your electrical and magnetic energies align.

If you cannot feel the desired emotion before the event occurs, no affirmation, no matter how often you repeat it, will manifest your reality. For example, if you want to feel happy when something happens but you can't feel that happiness until the event takes place, you are blocking the flow of energy necessary to draw that event into your reality.

Your thoughts—your electrical charges—send out an intention into the quantum field while your feelings—your magnetic charges—pull that intention back to you. If you wait for the event to trigger the feeling, you're missing the key ingredient: feeling it first. Without emotional alignment before the experience, you limit your ability to manifest. Evolution happens when thought and emotion are in perfect harmony, creating the energetic match required to bring about your desired reality.

AWAKENING

Awakening is a shift in consciousness, a profound transformation where you move from identifying solely with your physical body to recognising a deeper, soul-level connection with the divine, the universe or your higher self. It's an experience that deepens your sense of purpose, enhances your understanding of life and reveals the interconnectedness of all things. This shift illuminates a new perspective in which you see beyond the material and embrace the spiritual essence that unites everything.

An awakening occurs when you begin to shift your belief systems to align with a new version of yourself. You'll start to recognise what no longer serves you, and you naturally gravitate towards what does. This process often sparks deep introspection, causing you to question everything from the conversations you once enjoyed to the environments you once felt comfortable in. As your awareness expands, you might find that many things no longer resonate, and you'll feel the pull of something greater, something beyond the ordinary. Your mind will open up to new possibilities, and with that, a deeper understanding of life begins to unfold.

Opening Pandora's box means questioning everything you've ever believed, venturing into a tunnel of deeper knowledge. As we explore spiritual, scientific and philosophical teachings, we externalise our awakening until we face the concept of consciousness itself.

When you truly awaken, you'll realise that consciousness is everything. The moment you become fully aware of your thoughts and feelings, you'll see the exact beliefs that have kept you confined to a limited life. These beliefs are the walls holding you in a specific reality. Once you wake up to them, your desire for your old life will vanish. You don't need endless hours of research or podcasts—you have the power to instantly transform your life by facing the unconscious beliefs that are holding you back. If your life isn't changing, it's because you're still avoiding the belief that is keeping you stuck. Confront it, and your world will shift.

A mental cleanse is one of the most powerful and transformative things you can do, more vital than any academic skill. When you realise that no one can control your thoughts, you'll unlock the ability to shape your reality from within. Whether you're limited by your physical body, environment or circumstances, consciousness knows no boundaries. It's free, limitless and always available to you. As soon as you begin to think beyond the third dimension, you'll elevate your energy to a new realm where endless possibilities unfold. The world will truly become your oyster, and nothing can hold you back.

To be called crazy by those still trapped in the confines of societal and cultural conditioning is actually a compliment. It means you're thinking beyond their limits, questioning the world they accept without question. True freedom comes when you release yourself from the chains of linear time and space, when you stop living by the clock and start living by the beat of your own heart.

INTEGRATION

1. **Reflect on your dominant and recurring thoughts this week—write them all down.** How many stem from your current reality versus a deeper sense of self beyond external circumstances, possessions, or relationships?

2. **List three things you expect from your physical reality for external validation.** Identify specific things you seek from your environment or other people to affirm your worth, success or happiness. These might include validation from your job, your appearance, relationships, status, possessions or achievements.

3. **For each of these things, write down three affirmative beliefs you can instil in yourself regardless of the world around you.** Now, challenge yourself to write affirmations that empower you to feel whole, validated and successful without relying on external sources. Shift your belief system towards inner validation.

You Can Become The Creator

'You're only given a little spark of madness. You mustn't lose it.'

Robin Williams

A creator is someone who dares to step beyond the confines of society, beyond the rules that dictate what's possible, beyond the comfort of conformity. A creator breaks free from the chains of expectation, safety and limitation, refusing to be bound by what others deem 'realistic'. To be the creator of your life is to tap into an unshakable energy, a force that allows you to craft any possibility, no matter how **bold** or unconventional. It is the freedom to shape your own reality and live it on your own terms.

There are 8 billion unique belief systems, 8 billion perspectives, and 8 billion minds, each shaping life with the incredible power of thought. We come to Earth not just to exist but to use the energy of our beliefs, our attention and our minds to create. Just as an artist moulds clay with their hands, using the palms and pressure of their hands to sculpt the terracotta, you sculpt reality with your mind; your focus and intention become the force that shapes the world around you. Your mind speaks louder than any voice, feels deeper than any touch and is more powerful than any physical structure. Look around: everything that has ever been created was born from the belief that it was possible, and you, too, possess the life force and energy to create entire worlds, to reach new heights. When you realise that you are not the body but the soul that inhabits it, the body is not the source of your power but the vehicle through which your soul expresses itself, and everything outside of you becomes secondary.

Human potential is not determined by who you've been, where you come from or what you've experienced. It has nothing to do with your background, culture or circumstances. True abundance is born from how deeply you value yourself as a creator. A creator doesn't seek answers outside of themselves — they trust their inner wisdom, tapping into the boundless intuition that flows from within. You are the portal. You are the one who opens the doors, who chooses when to close them, who decides whether to leave them ajar or sealed tight.

When you seek proof from the outside world, you're still not tapping into your true power as a creator. If you find yourself asking, 'Where is it?' you're unknowingly doubting your own potential. It's okay to acknowledge external signs from time to time, but wouldn't it be more empowering to trust the strength within you? If you truly knew that you could create anything, you wouldn't question its arrival or doubt your own ability. If you believed you couldn't fail, there would be no limit to what you could be or do. You can't expect your life to transform if your environment dictates your thoughts and emotions. Recognise the creator within you, and you'll begin to respond to life with awareness and intention. It's not the events that cause unhappiness;

it's our belief in our ability to create. If you see yourself as a creator, you'll remain whole and empowered, even if everything around you seems to crumble.

A creator is someone who sees beyond the illusion of everyday reality, someone who knows, feels and senses that there is more to existence than just moving through routines, accumulating titles or checking off tasks on a to-do list. A creator understands that life is about love and fear, and despite the circumstances, always chooses love. When you embody this truth, nothing can stand in your way. If everyone recognised creation from this perspective, they would instantly realise their immense power, brilliance and worth.

Creating from a place of love means understanding that you arrived on this Earth already deserving, already worthy, already filled with love and ready to give and receive love. So, when you find yourself struggling to manifest your desires, recognise that it's not the lack of external resources that's blocking you but the absence of love within. Love is the force that holds everything together—without it, you'll doubt your ability to create, but when you fully love and believe in yourself, you'll realise that nothing is beyond your reach. You are already everything you need to be to create your deepest desires.

A true creator doesn't operate like a corporation following a rigid manual. A creator doesn't refer to a set of instructions, nor do they mimic someone else's path. Instead, they trust their own unique and powerful intuition to guide them. Creators can't be confined by rules, obligations or mechanical systems because these structures are based on linear thinking, while human potential is limitless. You are not meant to function within fixed parameters — you are meant to break free, to flow and to create authentically from within.

We often chase creation for external reasons, whether it's to possess more, become someone else, or simply to survive. Some strive for the glitter of success, others for basic security. We tend to reach for the external before we ever ask, *Who am I?* or *What do I truly want?*

But the truth is, everything in the physical world is linear, while the mind is infinite and multi-dimensional. Awakening is the moment you realise the outside world is merely a reflection of what's inside. There is no 'out there' without 'in here', no front without back, no light without dark, no joy without sorrow. When you understand that what you create in your inner world shapes the reality around you, that's when you can truly begin to shape a life that feels aligned with who you are and what you're meant to become.

Whatever you create, remember this: slowness is still progress, clouds without sun hold their own beauty, broken crayons still bring colour to the world, and light cannot exist without its shadow. True mastery in life is learning to trust with both heart and mind. Life isn't a race or a tally of gains — it's about recognising how intricate, intelligent and deeply detailed we are. You were never meant to be ranked from zero to 100, nor were you meant to climb some imposed hierarchy. You were meant to unfold at your own pace with the wisdom to know that every step, no matter how small, is still movement.

I look at myself now and wonder, how did I become the woman who wrote this book? How did I become the woman who walks into a bookstore or clicks on a link, selects my own book and adds it to my basket as casually as picking up groceries? How did I get here?

What is a book, what is a store, when I hold a mind of magic? This didn't happen by accident. It didn't happen without first believing that I could create something extraordinary, that I could shape my own reality with conviction and purpose.

INTEGRATION

1. **Imagine Yourself at 65.** Write a letter to your future self at 65. Describe your life in as much detail as possible: What might you believe about yourself at that age? What dreams or projects will you still be pursuing or have accomplished? What activities do you enjoy doing?

2. **'If I Had Money' — List of Stalled Wishes.** Think of five things you've always wanted to do but felt were out of reach, whether because of money, time or fear. Now, consider how you can make these happen today with the abundance that is already available to you in your life. Get creative! How can you work with what you have right now to make those dreams a reality?

3. **Limiting Beliefs and Empowering Affirmations.** List five things you do (or beliefs you hold) that stop you from truly believing you are capable of creating the life you want. Now, for each one, write down a powerful affirmation you can say to yourself daily to remind yourself that you *are* a creator.

You Can Bring Forth Your Final Vision

"And, when you want something, all the universe conspires in helping you to achieve it."

Paulo Coelho

You have an extraordinary gift: the ability to believe, feel and speak anything into existence. Do you truly understand how powerful you are? You were born to create, to manifest, to wield influence over your own reality. Yes, life can be chaotic at times, but that does not diminish your innate power. With this power, you have the ability to bring your deepest vision into being, starting right now.

Living your final vision today means paying attention to the small, everyday choices that shape your life. When you start making the decisions your future self would make *now*, you become that future version of yourself in this moment. Along the way, I've come to realise that in every moment, we are faced with two choices: to be a product of the past or a product of progress.

So, when you're walking to the Tube station frustrated and drained from another day at work, you can shift your perspective. Instead of dwelling in judgement and irritation, choose gratitude. You're part of the 1% who gets to go to work, to see, feel and move through the world. Instead of criticising the woman next to you for her outfit, recognise the abundance in both of you, both of you are covered, both of you are warm, both are rich in clothing and style. Your 'Why am I in this situation?' can be transformed into, 'This is the perfect place for me to be right now.'

You don't need external validation to prove that you can think, feel or act in a way that aligns with your highest self. Imagine waiting for an elevator. Instead of passing the time with impatience, wait with the excitement that whatever you've been waiting for is already waiting for you on the floor you're about to reach. As I write this book, I have the choice to focus on uncertainty, on where it might go, who it will reach, or whether it will ever be published, or I can shift my focus to gratitude. I can be thankful that I have the opportunity to put pen to paper, to channel my creativity into something tangible. When you approach life this way, you bend time and space, pulling your desired future into the present moment.

In this world, emotions are usually the result of our experiences, but if we want to truly feel whole, we must stop waiting for an external event or condition to fill us up. Feeling is essential to being, and to bridge the gap between who you are now and who you're becoming, you must start embodying the emotions you desire *before* an event even takes place. When you can feel the fullness of your vision before it manifests, you no longer need anything outside of you to define how you should feel or who you should be. Others may question, judge or doubt you, but if you remain steadfast in the power of who you're becoming, your reality will begin to shift in ways you can't yet imagine.

When you start embodying your desired future in the present moment, you'll release the feelings of desperation and lack that often accompany your desires. You'll no longer feel separated from your dreams. Instead of wishing for a perfect moment or waiting for ideal conditions, you'll realise that the only perfect time is now. It's time to pause and reflect—take a moment to list your non-negotiables for living your future **today**. What kind of thoughts, feelings and actions will your future self embody?

What beliefs will you hold? What energy will you carry with you?

This is the era to be unapologetically selfish. It's the time to put your own needs, desires and growth first. The world will always ask for your time, your energy, your attention, but what will you ask of yourself? It's not about neglecting others but about realising that you cannot pour from an empty cup. Prioritise your wellbeing, your dreams, your purpose. Be selfish for the sake of your soul.

When others witness your happiness expanding, your opportunities flowing in abundance and your life filled with rewarding and fulfilling experiences, they'll look at you and ask, 'What is it that you know that I don't?'

The one valuable thing you can offer them, the truth that will resonate deeply, is this: *'I am in true connection with myself.'* What you know is the key to everything they seek: the clarity to define who you are, what you feel, where you're headed and the life you're creating. *Now,* not someday. The truth you embody is power, and it comes from intentional living. Vagueness only creates confusion but clarity brings transformation, so be intentional in your thoughts, words and actions. With every choice, you take command of your life. No external force, 'evil eye' or negativity can steer you off course. When you live with this clarity, you are unstoppable. Your path and rewards remain yours alone.

Then, they'll ask, *'How do I get in connection with myself?'*

You'll answer, *'By being selfish.'* They'll frown. *'Isn't that bad?'*

You'll smile. *'No, because... '*

Being selfish is being in true alignment with your authentic self. When you vibrate at a higher frequency, you are connected to your true nature as a human being. This means *self* is positive, *self* is joyful, *self* is accepted, *self* is healthy, *self* is nourished, *self* is excited, *self* is grateful, *self* is abundant, *self* is balanced. So, if *self* feels anger, shame or fear, it's not selfish — it's a sign that something needs to shift.

Being selfish is the conscious choice to step away from anything that dims your authenticity. It's about intentionally training your mind to think positive thoughts and feel empowering emotions. Being selfish means setting boundaries with people, places, beliefs and past experiences. It's caring enough about your thoughts and feelings to become the greatest version of yourself. It's showing up for you—every time—when others are still deciding whether they should.

When you selfishly commit to your highest vibrational self, you simultaneously align with the greater good of humanity. The truth is, without a deep and unshakable connection to yourself, you have nothing to offer the world.

Now, let's say you've embodied this truth, and someone dares to criticise you. They'll say, *'You're so selfish, you only care about yourself.'* What they don't understand is that they're revealing their own weakness, an unwillingness to do the hard, uncomfortable work that only *they* can do for themselves. Instead of facing their own shadows, they want you to sacrifice your authenticity and do the work they're too lazy or afraid to take on. If they attack your selfishness, it's because they are stuck in their own mediocrity, too scared to step into the fire of their own transformation.

To be truly selfish is to become entirely selfless because you cannot pour into others if you have not first poured greatness into yourself. If you don't know what greatness feels like in your own bones, how could you possibly recognise it in anyone else? How can you lead with love if you haven't yet experienced the fullness of love within you? It is only when you've flooded your own being with boundless happiness and self-love that you can authentically show up to care for the world around you. It is only in filling yourself first that you unlock the true power to elevate others.

In this life, no matter what you face—whether it's you or the events around you—you are the one constant in every circumstance. That's why, above all, you must prioritise yourself today. Your well-being, your authenticity, your alignment with your true self—it's not negotiable. It's essential.

As you embrace your journey of selfishness, you will paradoxically become 100 times more selfless. By honouring your own needs, desires and boundaries, you cultivate the strength and abundance necessary to give more authentically and fully to others. True selfishness doesn't drain or isolate—it empowers and expands, allowing you to pour from a well that never runs dry. In nourishing yourself first, you become a source of limitless generosity for the world around you.

INTEGRATION

1. Reflect on how you spent your time this week. Did you prioritise yourself, or were you focused on external distractions? How much time did you spend procrastinating? Were you able to shift your mindset and let positivity lead, or did pessimism take the reins?

2. If you could live three different lives, who would you become? Review your list, then choose one persona to step into. This week, start integrating more of this life into your actions, thoughts and choices.

3. Revisit the list of lives you've created. If you feel inspired, add more possibilities to it. Once again, choose one to embody more fully in the coming week. Embrace this new aspect of yourself with intention and presence.

EPISODE 6

You Can Make Amends

'I learned [sic] a long time ago that some people would rather die than forgive. It's a strange truth, but forgiveness is a painful and difficult process. It's not something that happens overnight. It's an evolution of the heart.'

Sue Monk Kidd

Let's talk about **self-forgiveness,**

There's a powerful Hawaiian tradition called *Ho'oponopono* (pronounced ho-oh-po-no-po-no), a sacred practice of healing through forgiveness. It's not only a way to mend relationships with others but a profound journey to reclaim your own self-love, to restore the fractured parts of your soul and to rebalance the very essence of your being, your life, your spirit.

The word Ho'oponopono is a sacred call to restore balance, to bring everything back into harmony. This mantra is a cleansing ritual for the mind, body and soul, sweeping away toxic thoughts, painful memories and the dark weight of unkindness that can take root within us. Repeated with intention, it becomes a soothing melody in your inner dialogue, a reminder of what you need to hear when life feels off-beat. It creates space for you to honour the hurt, to acknowledge what went wrong and — most importantly — it delivers the healing antidote: forgiveness. It whispers *all is forgiven*, and in that moment, you are restored. This practice is both a call to presence and a shift in intention, unlocking the power of true forgiveness. When you confront your missteps, the world around you mirrors that shift. When you forgive yourself, everything else begins to forgive, too. Through this mantra, your heart opens to greater love, not only for yourself but for others, liberating your soul and revealing the boundless freedom within.

Dr Ihaleakala Hew Len is the visionary who introduced the Ho'oponopono healing method to the world. From 1983 to 1987, he served as a therapist at the Hawaii State Hospital, working in the ward for the criminally insane. The ward was a place of utter chaos, with staff members plagued by burnout, sickness and even resignation due to overwhelming, inescapable negativity, but Dr Len refused to accept this hopelessness. He chose a radically different path to healing, one that didn't involve directly treating the patients but rather, healing himself. He set up an office, reviewed each patient's file, and then immersed himself in meditation, repeating the four powerful mantras: *I'm sorry, please forgive me, thank you, I love you.* He never spoke to or interacted with the patients, yet over the next four years, every single patient was cured. The hospital, once overwhelmed with violence and despair, was eventually shut down, as there were no patients left. Dr Len's [8] extraordinary approach showed that when we heal ourselves, we heal the world around us.

Dr Len believed that total responsibility meant embracing the truth that everything in your life—every moment, every encounter—has always been a reflection of *you.*

---

8   *https://hooponoponomiracle.com/dr-ihaleakala-hew-len/*

Your reality is not a random sequence of events; it is the direct manifestation of your consciousness. To take full responsibility is to accept that everything you experience through your senses — every sight, sound and touch — is yours to own because it exists in your world. So, instead of viewing his patients as broken souls in desperate need of fixing, he faced the darkest parts of himself — the very aspects that had brought them into his life — and healed them from within.

The art of Ho'oponopono delves into the deepest core of how reality unfolds, unlocking the power to heal the very fabric of your life. You may be questioning, 'But Rania, how is it possible that just a few simple words could completely transform the lives of others?'

Well, Dr. Len understood that what we perceive as being 'out there' is never truly separate from us — it's all *within*. Instead of attempting to change the patients in his external world, he turned inwards, shifting his perception of them. In doing so, he transformed them because everything we encounter is merely a reflection of our inner world. When we alter how we see others, we step into an entirely new reality where healing is possible. Our interpretations, our beliefs, create the lens through which we experience the world, and through that lens, we shape everything around us.

The Ho'oponopono empowers you to reclaim your power from the external world you've allowed to define you. The four mantras hold an intense healing frequency because words are energy, unlocking the ability to dissolve the limiting beliefs, destructive patterns and judgements you've carried about yourself. Once you heal and shift the data stream within you, you step into full ownership of your life. Ho'oponopono grants you the clarity to peer into the very mechanics of reality, allowing you to confront and transform the hidden concepts, beliefs and energies that linger in your auric field. It's a deep dive into the unseen forces shaping your world.

I am sorry—These words are your declaration of ownership of the concepts you've created and brought into existence. You cannot transform what you refuse to claim as your own. By saying *I am sorry*, you acknowledge that all creation begins with your perception and interpretation of yourself and the world around you. You recognise that everything, no matter how it appears, is perfect as it is. The unhealed parts of you give rise to your beliefs and judgements, and through them, you shape the reality you experience. It is here, in this recognition, that you can take full responsibility.

Please forgive me—Forgiveness is the gateway to all healing. By saying these words, you release your judgement, your perception and your interpretation of everything you've brought into being. You begin to see that everything, as it is, holds its own perfect purpose. Nothing is wrong, nothing needs to change.

Thank you — With these words, you invite the powerful vibration of gratitude and completion. You express deep gratitude for the interpretations you once held, no longer judging yourself for them. You are thankful that these perceptions, even in their imperfection, have guided you toward higher consciousness, moving you forward on your path of healing and growth.

I love you — Love is the most sacred reflection of who we are, the very essence of existence itself. It is the foundation of reality, the force that connects us all. To live in love, to walk in love, is to align with the truest, most powerful frequency of the universe. It is the core of everything we are meant to be.

These words carry the profound truth that everything that has unfolded in your life is neither your fault nor anyone else's, but it is *entirely* your responsibility. The mantra calls you to purify your subconscious, clearing it of all toxic beliefs by harnessing the healing frequency within. As you do, these beliefs no longer project themselves into your 3D reality, transforming your world from the inside out.

RANIA HABIB

Forgiveness without conditions is essential because when you truly forgive, you free yourself to live in abundance, unburdened by any resistance. Forgiveness is not about backing down from your beliefs or showing weakness; it is the ultimate act of self-care, the one thing everyone needs. We often cling to the wrongs others have done to us, labelling and limiting ourselves and others by those past actions. We fall into the trap of believing that others must first make amends, that they must repair the harm they caused before we can forgive, but in holding onto this, we create conditions that keep us stuck and we waste valuable energy on these conditions that could be better spent creating something powerful and positive. If you truly want to live in abundance, let go. Forgive yourself and others in all their innocence and ignorance, and release the weight that keeps you from moving forward.

I invite you to take a moment to reflect on all the painful, hurtful relationships in your life. If you find yourself blaming others, know that you are still distant from your true self because radical self-forgiveness is about owning every relationship — every dynamic — that exists within you. It's about acknowledging the role you play in shaping your connections and understanding that true healing begins when you take full responsibility for your inner world.

True existence is not about operating from the ego because the ego doesn't seek growth; it clings to stagnation. Dwelling on what someone has done to you only feeds the cycle of resentment; this is the ego at work. Thoughts like *This should never have happened* or *They're so cruel* only attract more of what you don't want. At some point, you made a choice to operate at a certain level of consciousness, and while it may not have been your fault, it is now your responsibility to shift to a higher way of being and believing. Radical self-forgiveness is about taking full accountability for everything you are and everything you've been. The key is realising that your outer world is a mirror of how you think and feel about yourself. Everyone around you is simply playing their role in your story. Let go of all expectations of others, take it all into your heart, and ask:

- What within me, at that moment, attracted this into my life?

- Who was I *being* in that situation?

- How was I *feeling* deep down beyond the surface?

- What aspects of my self-concept need to be nurtured with more love and compassion?

The solution has always been within your mind. It's futile to try and change another person, to force them into the version you desire. As humans, we've been conditioned to believe that if someone isn't behaving the way we want them to, we must change them, but the truth of the reality is this: people simply mirror us, reflecting back that which we project. That's why it's crucial to tend to your mental diet because, if your self-concept isn't fulfilling, you won't be able to see fulfilment in others either.

To forgive yourself is to recognise that anything you dislike in your experience is simply a part of you that you have not yet fully loved. It's a call to embrace all of who you are without exception. When it feels like the world is falling apart around you, don't be deceived by appearances. Healing doesn't come from fixing what's broken — it comes from rising to new levels of consciousness, from expanding your awareness. Every challenge is an opportunity for growth, and everything is unfolding *for* you, not *against* you. Hold this truth close, especially in the darkest moments.

INTEGRATION

1. From the list of five people you've blamed during a time of hardship (from exercise two in *You Can Transcend the Victim*), repeat the Ho'oponopono mantra to each person again and again until you feel true forgiveness for them stirring in your heart.

2. Reflect on five moments when you struggled to forgive yourself. Becoming aware of these negative patterns allows you to dissolve them completely, breaking free from their grip.

3. Travel back in time to a moment when things were difficult. Write a letter of forgiveness to yourself, holding little you in your heart and offering the compassion you once needed but couldn't give.

You Can Heal Your Inner Child

'Everything seemed possible when I looked through the eyes of a child. And every once in a while, I remember I still have the chance to be that wild.'

Nikki Rowe

It took me years to realise that I am a reflection of my younger self in everything I say, everything I do and even in the places I choose to stay or leave. No matter how much I've grown, no matter how much I've changed over the years, that girl within me is still there, frozen in time. She remains stuck because there are parts of her that were never healed and never truly addressed.

If you don't confront your childhood traumas, they will echo through every area of your life. Your relationships, friendships, environments, joy and pain will all carry the weight of what's been left unspoken. It will manifest in every chapter of your story until you finally give voice to it. As long as you treat this pain as taboo, you'll live a life of restriction, constantly bound by the unaddressed wounds that shape your world.

The inner child is an inseparable part of you, like any organ that sustains you. It holds your imagination, your dreams, your visions, your purest qualities. It is the wellspring from which your personality traits flow. Healing your inner child means returning to the root, to the vessel you've neglected and rejected for so long, the vessel that has gathered dust, the one you keep reaching into without ever intending to truly heal. It's the part of you that holds the key to your deepest transformation.

The truth is, as young children, we are so full of life and wonder that our imagination knows no limits. We walk through the world spiritually free, light-hearted and unburdened, but more often than not, as we grow older, we are scolded for dreaming too big and for living larger than life. Rejection comes again and again because what we believe for ourselves doesn't fit into the 'realistic' box others try to place us in. In those moments of rejection, our younger, more vulnerable selves start to close off. The doors to our inner vessels, the ones that hold our most creative, playful and imaginative essences, begin to shut, and over time, those locks start to rust, leaving us trapped in cages of limitation.

The secret we fail to grasp as children is that, over time, we learn to reject the most authentic parts of ourselves, often because of external rejection and shame. As we grow, people around us instinctively try to shape us within the boundaries of their own beliefs and limitations. They project their consciousness onto us, pushing us to conform. Take a moment to reflect on your ten-year-old self—would your light have been brighter back then than it feels now?

Picture a mother and her child walking down the road—what do you see? The child leaps joyfully from one square to another, lost in an imaginary world, playing hopscotch on the pavement whilst the mother walks steadily, 'normally', because that's what society tells us adults should do. As children, we are free, unburdened and bursting with creativity, but somewhere along the way, we are taught to bury that light. Society and the system we've grown up in demand we reject the very parts of ourselves that are most alive. We are conditioned to let go of what makes us unique, what makes us shine—sometimes even parts of ourselves we never wanted to lose.

It's not fear that makes us give up our imagination as children—it's shame that comes when we are made to feel small, when others try to control how we think or act because it embarrasses them. For any child who was shamed—over their beliefs, their emotions, their behaviour—that shame doesn't just disappear when they grow up. It's carried and quietly festers, often without anyone there to enforce it, and if it's never confronted, that internal shame will quietly sabotage your adult life, holding you back from pursuing your deepest desires, from stepping into your fullest potential. Shame will steal your courage, keep you small and stop you from doing the things you truly long to do.

As a child, you may have been shamed for so many things: wanting attention, exploring something outside the norm, not meeting someone's expectations or even for the simple expression of your creativity; the list is endless. But when we are shamed as children, we are taught that it's wrong to think, feel or behave in certain ways. Beneath the surface of 'She forgot my birthday, but it doesn't matter' lies something far deeper: the shame that quietly lingers, waiting to attach itself to another part of your life. That very desire to feel seen and acknowledged on your special day? It's twisted into something shameful instead. That innocent yearning for connection and recognition becomes a burden you carry, whispering to you that you're not worthy of the attention or love you crave. That shame buried deep inside doesn't just vanish. It silently weaves itself into the fabric of who you become, affecting the way you show up in the world in ways you may not even realise.

Behind every ounce of shame lies the truth of who we *truly* want to be. This is why so many brilliant artists never exhibit their work, why incredible stories remain hidden beneath beds, why people with the most beautiful voices keep themselves silent. Shame silences us and keeps us small, and it doesn't end in childhood—it resurfaces in our adult lives because the inner child *never* leaves us. That child is the truest version of who we are, still longing to be seen, still bursting with untapped potential, but shame? The whispers of not being good enough or not belonging or being told not to stand out remind us to hide. They keep us from stepping into the fullness of our gifts, from sharing our hearts and our talents with the world, and so we stay small, muted, hidden as that inner child patiently waits for us to remember who we really are.

As an adult, it's crucial who you allow to give you feedback. Criticism from those who belittle, attack or mock your authentic self is damaging. Such shaming can lead you to shrink into a watered-down version of who you are. This doesn't mean avoiding feedback. It means protecting your truth. Learn when and from whom to seek guidance, and guard your inner child from unjust criticism. In doing so, you'll strengthen your ability to discern constructive feedback and stay rooted in your true self, even when faced with criticism.

The most important thing of all is learning how to self-nurture your inner child. This can mean allowing yourself to cry just as you did when you were a child. Remember how, as a child, crying was your first way to self-soothe, and it was pure. If you need to scream, sob or let out a primal cry, do it without shame. Expressing your emotions is a fundamental part of being human, and when you're ready, something inside you will shift, urging you to stop crying, not because the pain is gone but because you're stepping into a new chapter of releasing that shame once and for all.

If you ever catch yourself calling someone 'childish' for the way they live, pause and ask yourself why. It's likely that you're carrying shame about parts of yourself, the parts that once felt embarrassed and were hidden away, never to resurface. When you react to others, that's the shame inside you being triggered. A big part of healing is becoming aware of the language and judgements we direct toward others because they always reflect what's happening within us.

A key part of healing is to start playing again, laughing at things deemed 'silly' but that light you up inside. It's about imagining that the impossible is within your reach and embracing the boundless potential of your inner world. You have the power to create your own reality with your unique vision and joy. Play in a way that excites you because when you're filled with that childlike energy, you unlock a Pandora's box of endless possibilities.

When you experience intense negative emotions, it's crucial to dig deep and understand where they stem from. Often, it's your inner child running the show, simply craving more love. We are all shaped by an imperfect society and parents who, like you, are learning about life for the first time. Realising that my parents were navigating life as first-timers, just like me, shifted my perspective of them. Once you understand that we're all stumbling through this journey for the first time, you can't hold anger or resentment towards anyone.

By releasing the belief that we must be, behave or feel a certain way, we reconnect with the joy and playfulness of our inner child. We stop overthinking and simply *experience* ourselves, fully present, without judgement. Your inner child needs to be seen, heard and cared for, making them feel safe again. This responsibility falls solely on you. It's up to you to nurture yourself at every opportunity.

Once you reconnect with your childlike consciousness, you'll dissolve the blocks that once held you back from reaching your highest potential.

When you look in the mirror and see the person you've become, remember little you. They are the reflection of everything you are and everything they have taught you.

I look back at baby me and say thank you. Thank you for dreaming big, for wishing on stars and for allowing me to live this beautiful journey. If only you knew how truly beautiful you are, inside and out. I am in love with your hair, your smile, but most of all, the depth and goodness of your soul.

Don't be afraid to embrace your gifts—they will heal others and change the world. Trust yourself, trust your magic. You are far more powerful than you realise.

Here are six powerful ways to validate and comfort your inner child:

- Visualise yourself making eye contact with your inner child, lean in and give them a warm, loving hug.

- Speak the words to yourself now that you longed to hear growing up.

- Reassure your inner child that everything that happened wasn't their fault; they were just a child, never responsible for what occurred.

- Affirm that their feelings are valid; they were allowed to feel and express everything they did.

- Imagine you and your inner child in a safe space and tell them you are there for them, no matter what.

- Tell your inner child it's time to rest. You've learnt so much along the way, and from now on, you'll care for them every step of the journey.

INTEGRATION

1. Reflect on five traits you loved about yourself as a child.

2. Recall five accomplishments from your childhood, even something as simple as *I was kinder.*

3. List five people you felt safe with as a child. Reach out to them—a part of your healing is asking for support.

You Can Equate
Your Frequency

'Spread love everywhere you go. Let no one ever come to you without leaving happier.'

Mother Teresa

Albert Einstein once said, 'No problem can be solved from the same level of consciousness that created it.'[9] The solution lies above, on a higher vibrational frequency than the challenge itself. To shift your reality, you must elevate your consciousness to a different frequency. When you align with the frequency of the reality you desire by acting in your highest joy, you will step into that reality.

Frequency is the rate at which something occurs over time. When you hear the word 'frequency', think of it as how often you *be, feel* or *do* something. Everything in the universe—from the air we breathe to the solid objects around us—is made up of energies vibrating at different frequencies. Even what appears to be solid—like a rock or a chair—is simply vibrating energy on a quantum level.

Every thought, word, object, plant or grasshopper has its own unique vibration.

Frequency also applies to your thoughts and emotions because they are deeply intertwined. Thoughts create emotions, which, in turn, shape thoughts. When you think of something joyful, you naturally feel a wave of joy. Your mental and emotional states are constantly vibrating

9   *Elevate Society. (2023, May 21). No problem can be solved from the same level of consciousness that created it. (2023, May 21). https://elevatesociety.com/no-problem-can-be-solved/*

at a certain frequency, influencing how you experience and interact with the world around you.

For example, if you want to attract more abundance into your life, you must first be in a frequency where you are not desperate for it and where your current reality already feels full and complete. It may seem like a paradox, but abundance can't flow to you if you don't appreciate the abundance that already exists around you. True abundance enters when you no longer feel a sense of lack in your current circumstances. It's about knowing and feeling abundant *now*, not waiting and hoping for it to arrive.

Manifestation isn't about bringing something external into your life that you don't already have; no, it's about revealing what's already there, waiting for you by matching your frequency. If you're not in alignment with the vibration of what you desire, all the opportunities and gateways that exist for you will remain invisible. The only pathways you'll see are the ones that match your current vibration.

This awareness of your frequency will help you recognise what needs to be adjusted or attuned in order to align with the energy of what you want to manifest.

Dr Emoto[10] conducted an experiment in which he demonstrated that consciousness could influence the molecular structure of water. He exposed water to both positive and negative words, as these carry polar opposite energetic frequencies. Under a microscope, he observed that when love and gratitude were directed toward the water, beautiful snowflake-like crystals formed. However, when the water was exposed to hatred and negativity, its molecular structure became disordered and chaotic. These two experiences created two distinct types of consciousness. Now, you may be wondering how this applies to you. Well, since 70% of the human body is made up of water, the words, thoughts and feelings we direct toward ourselves can profoundly affect the structure of our cells, shaping our internal state and well-being.

The Schumann Resonance, often referred to as 'Earth's heartbeat', is a vital gauge of Earth's natural frequency, predicted by Winfried Otto Schumann in 1952. This frequency, 7.83 Hz, is the vibration sustaining and energising our planet. Interestingly, 7.83 Hz also aligns with alpha/theta brainwave frequencies in the human brain, in a state known for bringing about tranquil, energetic balance. In this state, cell regeneration and healing can occur. However, in recent times, Earth

---

10 *https://www.akwl.org/wp-content/uploads/2018/08/DrMorseEmoto.pdf*

has been bombarded by an avalanche of technological advancements, with external wavelengths disrupting her natural frequency. This imbalance has put us out of sync with the Earth's electromagnetic field. By tuning into the frequency of 7.83 Hz, we become more attuned to the healing benefits it offers, including enhanced memory, rejuvenated energy, reduced stress, improved mental clarity and a deeper sense of grounding.

On the 18th of June, 2023, the Schumann Resonance peaked at a staggering 190 Hz, a massive leap from its natural frequency of 7.83 Hz. This unprecedented shift marked the largest change Planet Earth has ever experienced, and if the Earth is evolving, we must evolve with it. If you're not actively working to align yourself with higher frequencies, life will gradually become more challenging. Your energy centres will no longer resonate with the frequency the Earth now operates at. Our minds, bodies and souls must be in harmony with Earth's new vibration. By resisting low-vibrational frequencies and nurturing higher ones, we can ascend alongside the Earth. This is the birth of the New Earth, where we transcend, evolve and become one with the planet's higher consciousness.

This is the essence of evolution: as you elevate your frequency, you create a new reality aligned with the highest potential of who you are meant to become.

MAGNETISM

Anything you can imagine or desire already exists as an energetic frequency, a potential reality waiting to be realised. Before something manifests physically, it exists first as an idea, a feeling or a possibility in the energetic realm. To bring that potential into the material world, you must align your own energy with it. When your vibration matches the frequency of what you wish to create, you bridge the gap between the invisible and the visible, turning possibility into tangible reality.

If you want to know which frequency you're operating at, simply look at what's being reflected back to you in the world around you. Everything you experience is a mirror of your current energetic state. Ask yourself: Who are you being right now? What language do you speak? What tone do you use?

What seat do you claim in life? What sensations fill your body? What intentions are driving you? Where is your focus? What choices are you making? Your new reality demands different answers to all of these questions. To shift your world, you must shift the frequency of who you are in this moment.

We have the power to draw things into our lives through the energy we embody rather than through frantic pursuit. Instead of living in a constant state of striving and chasing, magnetism nourishes a more effortless way of being. All the dreams and desires within your consciousness are only a frequency away. When you align yourself with the energy of what you want, you become a magnet, and everything you desire begins to draw towards you naturally. Just as flowers like the crocus, honeysuckle and wisteria effortlessly attract bees and insects with their vibrant energy or how the egg magnetises the sperm, everything you desire is waiting for you to simply *be* it. Like the begonias, standing tall in their magnificence, radiating their energy and sweet essence, you, too, can magnetise the life force that is drawn to you in perfect alignment.

True change begins within you long before your reality catches up. When you act differently—regardless of what your current circumstances look like—that's when you know you've changed. Change isn't about waiting for your external world to shift before you act; it's about aligning yourself first with the frequency of what you desire. Only then does your reality begin to reflect that inner shift. If you're waiting for the world to change first, you're still caught in the illusion that your circumstances determine who you are, but when you change—truly change from the inside—everything around you must follow.

ALIGNED ACTION

The true force behind action lies in the energy behind it. True movement comes only when your energy aligns with your desires. Once you're in that frequency, you'll know exactly what to do, where to go and what to say. The universe doesn't wait for you to catch up; it aligns with you when you align with it. Energy first, then action—**that's the flow of manifestation.**

If you can't access the 'how', or you can't find the steps or guidance, it's likely because you're not yet aligned with what you're after. You become magnetic to the ideas, opportunities and solutions when your frequency matches your desires. Many of us are waiting to feel good, loved, happy or truly alive, but the energy of waiting isn't receptive—it's repellent to what you desire on the other side.

Instead of waiting, here's the formula for raising your vibration:

1. Act on your highest excitement.

2. Keep going until you can't anymore.

3. Let go of attachment to specific outcomes.

4. Stay positive, no matter what happens.

5. Explore your beliefs, release old stories and release fear and negativity.

When you feel excitement or a surge of love and creativity, it's a signal, a reminder of a passion within you. These emotions are the frequency of your true self, the vibration of who you authentically are.

Taking inspired action doesn't always have to be monumental. It can be as simple as finding moments of joy in your everyday life. Life can get consumed by tasks and objectives, but the key is to infuse your day with small actions that spark excitement even in the slightest. If you're unsure where to start, look at your current options and choose the one that brings the most joy, however small. If that matcha from the coffee shop lights you up more than the one you make at home, then go for it. It's not about the big things—it's the small moments of excitement that, over time, align you with your true frequency. Act on it without expectations and continue as long as it feels right. The energy of that joy will guide you. When you follow even the smallest spark of excitement, you ignite a powerful wave of momentum that draws more magic into your life.

How do you know if you're truly acting on your highest excitement?

Sometimes, what feels like 'excitement' is just your unconstructive ego trying to convince you that it's bliss. If you take a step back and listen closely, you may feel the underlying unease and apprehension beneath the surface. If anxiety or discomfort lingers, it's likely the ego tricking you into thinking that unease is excitement. To take it further, look at your physical reality, as it will always reflect the truth. The ego's illusion can only last so long before your reality shows you something's out of alignment.

Another sign that your excitement may not be genuine is when something seems exciting, yet you find yourself reacting negatively to the circumstances around you. This is a clear sign that it's not true excitement but a hidden negative belief pattern at play. Your task is to ensure that your highest excitement aligns with what you experience in your physical reality. If there's any misalignment, it's time to dig deeper and reassess what you truly felt excited or joyful about. Ultimately, it comes down to how you respond to what's happening around you, whether you respond with genuine excitement or simply mask fear.

TRIGGERS

It's no surprise that when we see others showing different sides of themselves—whether it's their success, confidence or achievements—we can feel triggered. In those moments, we might react from a place of discomfort, wanting to pull away, compare, criticise or somehow diminish what they're showing us. When we feel triggered by the full expression of others, it often stems from the fact that we've repressed parts of ourselves. Those parts feel foreign, unfamiliar and hard to accept.

A trigger is a mirror to something inside you that's still waiting to be expressed. It's a desire, a wish or a part of you that's been left dormant. It's the belief that what others are doing or having is somehow out of reach for you. When you're triggered, you witness a disowned part of yourself, the version of you that you're not allowing to fully come forward.

So, here's another truth: people are here to show you the many ways you can expand. They're not here to trigger you because you're not a victim. Every person you encounter, every interaction is an opportunity for growth and transformation. What they reflect back to you is not a threat but a chance to recognise the parts of yourself that are ready to evolve. When you embrace, embody and express the parts of yourself you've repressed, you'll no longer judge those same parts when they appear in others. If you're triggered, it's a sign that you're not yet fully free.

People are constantly showing you, guiding you and speaking to you in subtle ways to support your growth. They're here to inspire the hell out of you, to help you reclaim the parts of yourself you've disconnected from and to lead you into a life of abundance and overflow. Through them, you discover the inner work you need to do, the questions you need to ask and the emotions you need to feel. Pay attention to what you desire when others are living your dream. Notice the beliefs you need to adopt by observing what others believe about themselves. Notice the feelings you need to embody by feeling what others feel about themselves. When you focus on the lack of what hasn't happened for you yet, you miss a powerful invitation to expand.

When something unexpected or undesirable shows up in your life, remember this: even in the face of hardship, the only reason it's here is to expand you. Anything that enters your reality—no matter how difficult—can be used to propel you forward, even if it initially feels gut-wrenching. Make it your practice to transform these moments into opportunities to clarify what you truly want, allowing you to become even more intentional with your thoughts and emotions. The key is to rise above the frequency of what you don't prefer. Each time you rise above, you tap into new potential. Recognise that when you sit in sorrow, you're aligning with the frequency of that sorrow, and in doing so, you'll only attract more of it. This is your invitation to rise—again and again—into a higher frequency, where growth and transformation await.

When you see others, remember: *there is only one you*. The world needs you to show up as yourself, not as a copy of anyone else. Even if you tried, you could never replicate their journey. The world wouldn't allow it. If someone else has created what you desire, trust that *your version* will always be different and uniquely yours. There is room for you and the other 8 billion people. People are calling you to rise, to repeat greatness and to expand. They are healing you, showing you possibilities you haven't yet seen. Stop seeing others as competition or threats. See them as mirrors reflecting your own potential, urging you to step into your greatness. You are meant to inspire, not be inspired by fear. Let them show you who you're becoming.

The more you embrace your authenticity, the more you become an expander, someone who uplifts and inspires those around you. This is the beauty of life: it always comes full circle. When you show up as your true self, you create a ripple effect that empowers others to do the same, and that energy returns to you in ways you can't even imagine.

From now on, refuse to align with the frequency of anything you don't prefer. Be mindful of the labels, beliefs and definitions you assign to circumstances. When faced with challenges, redefine them instead of accepting them as 'obstacles'. Remember, existence is nothing more than a collection of perspectives, opinions and beliefs, each of which you have the power to transform.

INTEGRATION

1. Your frequency can be influenced by those around you. List the family and friends who uplift and nurture you, not the ones you 'need', but the ones who reflect your potential and possibilities.

2. Pause for a moment. Look around and identify five things in your environment that fill you with gratitude. Make these five reminders your daily focus, anchoring you in appreciation.

3. Write down anything that triggers anger, resistance or upset within you. Dive deeper to uncover the hidden insecurity behind these feelings. Beside each one, write: 'For every problem, there is a solution.'

You Can Manifest

'You cannot swim for new horizons until you have courage to lose sight of the shore.'

William Faulkner

With an overwhelming flood of information at our fingertips, manifesting has become more confusing than ever. Since the manifestation craze spread globally, countless techniques and 'secrets' have flooded the scene, often distorting the true essence of what manifestation truly is. Once you realise that it's not about obsessively chasing material possessions or desperately seeking love, you'll begin to understand the real power of manifestation. It's not external—manifestation is an inside job.

Manifesting is not something you do, nor is it something outside of you. Manifestation is you. You don't manifest *things;* you are the manifestation.

The obsession with 'bulletproof' manifestation techniques has shifted the focus from the true source of power—your state of being. When you desperately jump from one method to another, hoping one will work, you only deepen the sense of lack and distance from what you truly desire. Each time a technique doesn't yield results, you move on to the next, unknowingly creating from a place of scarcity. Yearning and obsessing over something only reinforces the belief that you are incomplete without it. As long as you focus on the absence, you stay separated from your manifestation.

Techniques, methods and step-by-step guides don't manifest—we do.

The universe doesn't give you what you want; it gives you who you are. It doesn't respond to your cravings but to the energy you embody. It doesn't deliver anything outside of your thoughts, beliefs and feelings because that is the frequency you're putting out.

The principles of energy tell us that energy is neither created nor destroyed, which means that what you desire already exists. Your only job is to align with its vibrational frequency through your state of being. If you truly understood your power, you'd silence the thoughts that keep you from the life you want. If you knew your own strength, you'd already be living your dream life.

Your 'I AM' shapes your life's journey. Life is about finding laughter where you've cried, smiles where you've screamed, and growth where you've once felt restricted. It's about alchemising your story at every turn, transforming each moment to be better than the last.

Eckhart Tolle said, 'When you create a problem, you create pain. All it takes is a simple choice, a simple decision: no matter what happens, I will create no more pain for myself. I will create no more problems.'[11]

- Be the person who already has what you want through your thoughts and feelings.

- Immerse yourself fully in the experience of being the version of yourself who lives in that desired reality now.

- Embody that version before the physical evidence appears.

- Your imagination is the key to manifestation. By embracing its power and focusing on the fulfilment within, you can release the need to react, chase or rely on external circumstances.

You are already an incredibly powerful manifester. The fact that you're experiencing a reality and are reading this book proves that you know how to manifest. If you didn't, you wouldn't have any reality to experience at all. Manifesting, attracting and creating is something you do all the time, whether consciously or unconsciously. The real question isn't *How do I manifest better?* but *Why am I manifesting what I'm experiencing?*

---

11 *Tolle, E. (n.d.). Eckhart Tolle > Quotes > Quotable quote. Goodreads. https://www.goodreads.com/quotes/9724716-when-you-create-a-problem-you-create-pain-all-it*

When you understand your *why*, you'll become more intentional and clear about what you truly want through the process of redefinition. The root of it all lies in your unconscious belief systems. By becoming aware of the deeper reasons behind what you're experiencing and redefining them, you shift the trajectory of your reality. If you no longer wish to experience something, you must change your beliefs around it.

Awareness of your beliefs is a choice you make for yourself. If you say you want change but don't examine your belief systems, then you're not truly ready for the transformation.

INTEGRATION

1. List five of your secret dreams: 'I secretly want to be a ____.'

2. In your current life, what beliefs or feelings can you lean into more deeply that will bring you closer to your dream?

3. List five façades or masks you're ready to let go of in order to pursue your true dream.

You Can Focus On Your Fruit

'Life is always now.'

Eckhart Tolle

Presence is beyond currency, and its worth is unquantifiable.

I used to have endless conversations with myself about the person I wanted to become as I grew older. I couldn't wait to get older—everything about it felt like an adventure waiting to happen. The thought of thinking older thoughts, doing older things and being free in ways that only adults could be was exhilarating. I was always in a hurry. My age told me to line up my dolls, invent their stories, mimic their voices, but all I wanted was to watch TV shows about teenagers being teenagers. I counted down the days until I would finally be 'free', thinking that adulthood was the key to the freedom I craved—no one to tell me when to sleep, where to go or what to wear.

And yet, a decade later, there I was, trapped within the walls of corporate life. I became a prisoner of my own creativity, choking on a dream that once felt so real, so close. I yearned for the scent of freedom I could have touched ten years ago but didn't. When I look back now, all I can see is how I spent my time wishing, waiting and dreaming, completely oblivious to the power of the present moment. The truth was that I was too busy waiting to live, not realising that I was already living in the moment I'd longed for.

As you navigate through the countless paths and dreams that pull you in every direction, know that there is always motion. Nothing halts, and nothing waits for you. Everything is in constant flux: streams transform into rivers, caterpillars evolve into butterflies, and bricks become towering buildings. The universe brims with infinite possibilities, all unfolding in real-time. Every single moment rests within your grasp, and it is always, without exception, up to you how you respond, how you move and how you create.

When you fully honour the present moment, embracing everything that is, you open yourself to receive more. In each moment, you face a choice: to resist and reject the energy around you or to flow with it, accepting it as perfect as it is. The more you cultivate gratitude for what is right now, the more you lay the foundation for everything you aspire to create. The 'future' never truly arrives as something separate; it only unfolds as the present. To be truly grateful is to value and cherish the moment you're in without comparison to a past that no longer exists. Gratitude is not about looking back and wishing for more; it's about fully embracing and appreciating all you have *now*. This is the magic that shapes everything to come.

The present moment is the key to everything, your gateway to infinite possibilities. If you're constantly anchored in the past or chasing the future, the things you seek will remain elusive. They can't find you because they only exist in the **now,** a place you're never in. If what you desire isn't aligning with you, perhaps it's because you're not truly living in the present, where all the wonderful opportunities you need are right in front of you. The moment you're in is where everything you need resides. Embracing the fullness of *now* will guide you exactly where you're meant to be. If you wait for the perfect moment, you'll be forever waiting.

Society teaches us to constantly prepare for the next moment, convincing us that the future holds more value than the present. We're trained to think that by obsessing over what's coming next we're getting ahead but, in reality, this mindset causes us to miss the beauty and power of *now.* The present moment is the only time that truly exists, and if you find yourself waiting or wishing for something else, you're missing out on life as it unfolds. Fear of the future often distracts us from the abundant power we hold in the present. When you release fear and stop letting it govern your thoughts, you'll start to live fully in the moment, knowing deep down that everything always works out, and often, it unfolds in ways even better than you imagined.

If you truly stop and reflect, every moment, every minute that passes is gone forever. From the curve of your smile to the Earth's quiet, daily exhale, each is as alive as the other. Until you realise that life is one continuous *now*, a series of present moments woven together, you'll feel as though life is simply happening to you, and you'll call it destiny. When you fixate on a time that doesn't exist, chasing a future outcome, you only keep feeding a loop of unfulfilled potential, a vortex that never materialises. The more you chase, the more you miss the magic of the present, where everything truly happens.

We've become so accustomed to doing that we forget the power of simply being. We often believe that when we're not physically engaged in activity, we're wasting time, but at our cores, we are human *beings*, not human *doings*. If we want happiness, we must be happy *now*, not as a future goal. If we crave freedom, we must be free in this moment. If we seek love, we must embody love. If we long for abundance, we must radiate abundance. It's not about wishing, hoping or waiting—it's about practising the essence of what we desire and *becoming* it first.

When we're not *being*, we're often excusing ourselves, waiting for better circumstances, better people, better situations as if we need something external to make us whole. But the truth is, there is nothing to wait for because what we're waiting for doesn't exist in the future—it's already here. Stop waiting for a specific set of conditions to become what you wish to be. The past is gone, the future is yet to unfold, but now — the present — is the only moment of true possibility.

I've spent so much of my life on pause, telling myself I'd start living once my skin cleared up, or when I was thinner or when I had more money or when I felt braver. I kept waiting for the 'right' moment, but the truth was that I was standing at a stop where the bus never arrived. The years passed, and everything around me was moving except for me. I was waiting, stuck in a loop of indecision because I didn't trust myself to take action. If I didn't trust myself *now*, why would I trust myself later? I played it safe, hiding behind daydreams, telling myself that *someday*, things would fall into place, but nothing ever happened, not even when I obsessed over a flicker of potential. I wasted my present, thinking that the perfect moment would eventually come. What I wish I'd known earlier is this: The *right* time is now. The present moment is always the best starting point, even when everything isn't perfect.

YOUR WAITING SEASON

The universe often places us in what feels like a 'Waiting Season', but we tend to misinterpret it. We think it means waiting for marriage, waiting for the perfect partner, waiting for a baby, waiting for a house, waiting to overcome depression, waiting for the right opportunity to manifest, waiting for more money or waiting for the new year. We're always on the lookout for the *right* person or the *right* circumstance to show up, but nobody shows up as the right person or the right circumstance until we decide to be the right person right now.

If you find yourself in a Waiting Season, ask yourself:

- What am I waiting for? And more importantly, what am I *becoming* in this waiting?

- What am I not choosing to embody right now that could shift everything for me in the present moment?

- What is this moment teaching me?

- What lessons do I need to take with me from this season?

- What do I need to overcome, unlearn and release in this very moment?

Your Waiting Season is where the unseen work happens, where you transform, expand and become the person you didn't know you were capable of being. Endurance, faith, resilience — these qualities can only be born through the challenges and stillness of these seasons. Instead of allowing yourself to sit in frustration or self-pity (which is okay for a brief moment), ask yourself, *How can I wait well?*

Waiting doesn't have to mean stagnation. It's a chance to deepen your connection to the present moment, nurture your inner strength and prepare yourself for the next chapter. The way you wait shapes the way you'll show up when it's time to move forward.

The present moment never asks you to wait without purpose. Every moment you are given holds something deeper, a lesson or a shift in the making, but to receive it, you must stop reaching for the past or scrambling towards the future. Sometimes, when you want something desperately, it seems to elude you, and that's because there's something more important for you to harvest first. Just as crops need time to grow, so, too, do the conditions in your life need to be right for what you desire to flourish.

Your Waiting Season is not about doing nothing; it's about refining your inner self to match the person you must become to receive what you're asking for. The universe doesn't operate in the way you expect it to—it knows you better than you know yourself. If your prayers aren't being answered right now, know that you are living in the manifestation of prayers you made before, and those wishes will come in exactly the way they are meant to.

When the things you've asked for finally arrive and they don't look the way you imagined, trust that they've come to you in the best form possible. Life always works to benefit you. When you cultivate a deep trust in this truth, nothing that happens will seem like an obstacle. Risks won't feel threatening because you'll know they're leading you exactly where you need to go.

Your desires will demand the release of your old habits. If you find yourself constantly wondering why you can't reach your goals, it's because they cannot manifest while you're bound to the old patterns that no longer serve you. Every time you try to chase something new whilst holding onto the old, you're building walls between where you are now and where you want to be, but the moment you consciously pull yourself back into the present, you reclaim control. You break the cycle. You silence the noise from past emotions and old conditioning that have kept you running in circles. By returning to the now, you free yourself from the energetic bonds of your past, creating the space needed for something new to take root.

It's a practice, a continuous act of returning to the present. Each time you do this, you access a fresh well of energy, one that is not burdened by what was but is open to what is and what can be.

In the quiet moments of solitude you find, honour how sacred they truly are. Let them be a space to sink deeply into the love you have for yourself and the world around you. Use that time to merge with the magical thoughts that uplift you, allowing the noise of the outside world to fade into the background. Come back home to yourself whenever you can, plunging into the peace that exists in that very moment. Know that, right now, nothing is missing, and everything is unfolding perfectly.

When you're waiting—whether for your morning coffee or for the slow load of an Excel sheet—take a moment to look up. Look at the sky, look back to yourself and to the dreams you feel you're struggling to keep up with. Remember, the dream is not out there in the future—it's alive now, in this very present, woven into the fabric of the cosmos, exactly as it should be.

INTEGRATION

Each day, dedicate time to journal anything that's on your mind. Don't overthink it — write whatever comes up, even if it's as simple as 'I stink.' Think of this as a listening exercise to tune in to what's happening in your mind right now. Whether you jot down a few sentences or fill ten pages, it's all perfect for you in that moment. What you write is exactly what you need to express in order to clear space and understand where you are today. This practice is a powerful tool for self-awareness, allowing you to check in with your thoughts and feelings and let them flow freely. Trust that whatever comes out is exactly what needs to be heard.

You Can Redefine Your Past

'I have great respect for the past.'

Maya Angelou

It's never too late to reinvent and redefine who you are. Right now, in this very moment, you can decide that everything you've been up until now is irrelevant. You can choose to step into a new life, a new version of yourself, because your past only defines you if you allow it to. Your future is yours to create, and it starts with the choices you make *right now*.

Don't let your future dreams, excitement and happiness be sabotaged by the comfort of familiar choices, chaos and fear. The secret to creation lies in pouring all your energy into building the new, not fighting against or proving the old.

Tony Robbins, author, coach and motivational speaker, wisely points out that the biggest conflict humans experience on a daily basis is the need to remain consistent with how they choose to identify themselves. The need to stay consistent is usually what forces people to stay stagnant and stuck. There is so much peace in knowing that just because you did something one way for a long period of time, this doesn't mean you have to keep doing it that way. [12]

---

12 *Robbins, T. (n.d.). Tony Robbins, Sage, and Mary B. on Expanding Your Identity. Tony Robbins. Retrieved from https://www.tonyrobbins.com/podcasts/identity*

To redefine who you are, you must redefine how you act and what you believe is possible for you. The only thing holding you back is your attachment to the 'old you', and that's something you can release at any time.

If you do not redefine and release the past, it will continue to define you.

How does the past define you?

The past will continue to define you if you keep repeating the same stories, clinging to the same feelings and acting from the same old patterns. By holding onto those familiar narratives, you bind yourself to a version of the past that no longer serves you. As long as you identify with those outdated patterns, you remain anchored in a cycle that limits your growth. Growth happens when you choose to release those attachments, allowing yourself to step into a new story, one that is aligned with who you are becoming, not who you once were.

By redefining your beliefs, you transform your past into great wisdom, but this transformation cannot happen while you're still holding onto the pain, still consumed by the thoughts and emotions that keep you chained to old stories. Sometimes, awakening feels unbearable because the grip of attachment to certain thoughts, feelings, and outcomes is too strong to release. It's easier to stay in the familiar, even if that familiarity is chaos and conflict, because it's what has kept you 'alive' up until now, but true growth requires courage. Redefinition means embracing the painful chapters of your story, not as burdens but as catalysts for your evolution. The real question isn't whether it happened to you, but whether you can see it as happening *for* you, as the universe's tough-love push to help you step into your higher self.

You don't redefine your beliefs by repeating empty affirmations like, 'I am divine love, I am divine love, I am divine love,' for ten minutes a day. That's not how transformation works. Your energy is better spent digging into the *why* behind your beliefs. As human beings, we hold on to beliefs because we think they serve us in some way, whether consciously or unconsciously. The moment you become aware of a belief that no longer serves you, naturally, you don't need to fight it or repeat mantras to mask it—you simply *let it go*. It's just like no longer liking a jumper you once liked. The power lies in awareness. Once you see the belief for what it is you can release it, and in that release, you create space for a new belief to emerge, one that's aligned with your true power and potential. It's about dismantling the old programming so the new can take root.

We go through hurdles, challenges, arguments and feelings of unworthiness until, one day, our eyes close, and we're gone. Think about that for a moment: how many of us are walking through life not truly *living* but simply *surviving*? We've advanced technologically, but in so many ways, we've spiritually devolved. We're caught up in the noise of what needs to be done tomorrow, who said what, or what didn't go as planned, but, just for a second, pause. Let go of everything: all the tasks, the stress, the worry. Forget it all. Now, ask yourself, *Is this the life I want to live? Is this the life I've been waiting for, working for, fighting for?* We are so caught up in the whirlwind of doing that we forget the power of simply *being*. Don't wait until the end to realise the only thing that truly matters is the present moment, the life you're living right now.

The past cannot block your happiness today.

Happiness is not a destination — it is a state of being. It's a habit you build, a muscle you strengthen with each choice you make, and the beauty of it is that *you* hold the power to choose it again and again, moment after moment.

Every day, every hour, every breath you take is an opportunity to choose happiness. Even on days when it feels distant or elusive, *choose it anyway*. Choose to see the beauty in the ordinary, choose to be present in the now, and choose to be grateful for all that you already have.

When you wake up each morning, remind yourself that you are alive. You have food, shelter, warmth and health. Your body is a miracle in itself: your heart beats, your lungs breathe, and you have the ability to feel, to move, to think. The vast majority of the world doesn't have what you have in this very moment. You are already so incredibly blessed.

Happiness isn't a luxury—it's your birthright. The more you lean into it, the more it becomes a part of who you are. It becomes the way you see the world, the way you redefine your past, the way you experience your life, and the way you show up for yourself and others. So, choose happiness. Choose it when you wake up, choose it when you face challenges, and choose it when you get lost in the everyday hustle.

Happiness has always been an inside job. It's the quiet strength of learning to love yourself exactly as you are and seeing the beauty in every step of your journey, and in that love, you'll find everything you've been searching for.

INTEGRATION

1. Reflect on all the insights shared in this episode and take a moment to redefine your eleven-year-old self. What was your heart like back then? What dreams did you carry? How did you see the world, and how did the world see you?

2. Transform your environment in a way that feels healing to you. Whether it's clearing away what no longer serves you or bringing in something that nurtures your soul, make space for change in your surroundings.

3. Write a journal entry from the perspective of your *new past*. What would your life look like right now if you had been nurtured in a different way? How can you gently reparent yourself today, offering the care and love you may have missed?

You Can Let Go Of The Future

'What we have is enough for us. Once we adopt that style of living, we become a happy person right away.'

Thich Nhat Hanh

The future is a place that hasn't yet been born. It is an illusion, a construct of our minds that pulls us away from the only real moment we ever have—now. When you keep living in it, you deny yourself the chance to truly live.

If you're consumed by endless thoughts of the future, you'll never experience the essence of life today. A lotus doesn't say, 'I'll wait until summer to give my fragrance,' it cannot help but bloom and give its fragrance in every season. It doesn't decide to share it only with happy people or deny it from the sad. It gives freely simply because that is its nature. The moon doesn't say, 'I'll only shine on the happy,' nor does the tree say, 'I'll wait until summer to give oxygen,' they simply are. The lotus always smells sweet, the moon always shines brightly, and the tree always provides oxygen.

They don't withhold their fullness based on conditions. They don't wait for the right moment to be their true, abundant selves.

Nature doesn't make mistakes and neither should you. Why wait for the perfect conditions, whether that's more money, a better season, or more love? Why only give love to those who love you back?

Nature doesn't limit itself like that, and neither should you. You are meant to be full in this moment as you are, without waiting for anything to change.

When you're lost in a daydream of who you want to become, what you want to feel, or what you want to have, you're not truly living—you're just surviving. Your breakthrough will come when you realise that the future only ever arrives as the present moment. From that point forward, the future isn't some far-off place, but it's something you create now. When you fully embrace the power of the present, your today will be the future you once longed for and waited on.

Regret has become a generational pattern because we've learnt to wish away our time, endlessly fantasising about the 'future best version of ourselves', while completely neglecting the incredible potential we have to contribute, be and do right now. When we constantly visualise where we want to be without acknowledging the power of becoming that version today, the gap between who we are and who we wish to be grows wider and wider until it feels unreachable. The truth is, the importance of today far outweighs any distant vision of tomorrow. This very moment is the foundation that leads to greatness. You may never recall this moment again, but today is the building block that keeps you standing tall, aligned and moving in the direction you desire.

If you wait or wish for the future, you must learn how to wait and wish well. There's a significant difference between waiting with intention and simply waiting in stagnation.

True faith doesn't just wait; it prepares. It nourishes the soil, waters the path and sets the stage for what is to come. The reason what you're waiting and wishing for hasn't arrived yet is because it can't find you; you're not fully present. Everything you desire exists right now in this infinite present moment because it's the only time that truly exists. If you're not here in the now, you will miss it every time, so if you find yourself waiting or wishing, ask yourself, 'Where am I?' If you're not in the present, bring yourself back to the only place that truly matters.

Sometimes, we find ourselves out of alignment with the very star we've been wishing on because we're showing up in ways that are too rigid and too controlled. We become fixated on one path — Route A — believing it's the only way but in reality, Route Y is the one that's always been destined for us. Route Y is the one that will exceed every expectation, the one that will bring you 10 times more than you imagined, but because we're so locked into the confines of A, we miss it. Our living space feels so limited, yet the universe has a whole expanse waiting for us to step into. When you release the rigid expectations of how things 'should' unfold, you'll be met with something far greater than you ever dreamed of. It's about releasing all expectations to unlock the door to a reality far beyond your current vision.

Life isn't a one-size-fits-all journey. Some people are meant to take the back roads, others may glide down peaceful country lanes, and you, perhaps, will find yourself on a one-way street for a while, but the truth is, right now, you're spoiled with options. You have countless paths, passageways and crossroads ahead of you. The beauty lies in the freedom of choosing which direction to go. You must remember: no matter how many times you feel re-routed or uncertain, every step you take is a step towards exactly what you need. Your compass today is guiding you where you're meant to go, and each turn is unfolding for you, not against you.

When life gets hard and the weight of the future feels heavy, know this: you're not being punished; you're being created. Every challenge, every moment of uncertainty, is shaping you into something greater than you imagined. The struggles you're facing are not signs of defeat—they are the forge, the fire, that is moulding you into your truest form.

Once you recognise the power of the present, you'll no longer drift aimlessly, speak without intention, or get lost in overthinking the future. You'll show up entirely aware that each moment holds the potential to shape your reality. No more wasting time on what-ifs or maybes; you'll be anchored in the now, knowing that this is where life happens.

INTEGRATION

1. Whether it's winter or summer, imagine what you'd do in the opposite season. If it's cold, dream of a warm, sunny day, and if it's hot, picture a crisp, cool breeze. Plan a perfect day that matches the opposite climate and go live it this week—rain or shine, don't let anything hold you back. There are no limits to your experience.

2. Write down five goals you want to achieve this year. What can you do today to move closer to one of them? Even a small step will bring you closer to making it happen sooner.

3. Incorporate this affirmation into your morning routine: 'I am who I am, and that is enough.' Let it sink in deeply as you start your day, reminding yourself that your essence is already perfect, just as it is.

You Can Compute Your Fears

'When your dreams are bigger than the places you find yourself in, sometimes you need to seek out your own reminders that there is more. And there is always more waiting for you on the other side of fear.'

Elaine Welteroth

I've always longed for a world where fear is no longer a shadow we hide from but a raw, unfiltered truth we can confront without shame. The moment I stopped running from it, when I finally let myself feel it fully, I saw it for what it truly was: an empty, fragile illusion. It lost all its power. It became nothing. And I'm here to guide you through that exact transformation, to help you shatter the illusion of fear, strip it of its power and watch it crumble before you. No more hiding. No more silence. Just raw, fearless freedom.

Fear is not some monstrous, uncontrollable force — it's actually a messenger, a signal that your belief system is misaligned with your true self. It's telling you that there's a thought, a belief, an idea that no longer serves you that is standing in the way of your authentic power. If you face it directly, you'll discover exactly what those beliefs are, and in doing so, you'll have the opportunity to let them go.

Fear only holds its grip as long as you remain unaware of the belief behind it. The moment you become conscious of it, you gain the power to choose something new.

Fear is the anchor holding you in place, preventing any forward momentum, stifling your growth and potential. I invite you to step into a new space, a space where you change your relationship with fear.

If you haven't already realised, fear is a silent thief, stealing the very life you're meant to live. It holds you back from becoming the greatest version of yourself that's just waiting to emerge. It stops you from speaking your truth, from writing the words that need to be said, from facing the emotions that are begging to be released and from taking the actions that will set you free. Fear convinces you that staying small is safe and that staying stuck is secure, but in reality, it traps you in a loop of stagnation. You may not even see it, but when nothing in your life changes, when nothing develops or moves forward, it's because fear has you roped to the past. It's time to recognise it for what it is—a barrier, not a shield—and break free.

One day, you'll make an unbreakable vow to yourself that the next time fear shows up, you will stand tall, rise above it, and conquer it without hesitation.

The belief that you need protection because of your fear *invites* the attack. Let that sink in. If you've been following along so far, this will resonate deeply. Don't cower from the belief. Don't run away from it in fear. Choose a new belief and *run toward it* with joy. Do you feel the shift? Do you still believe in the 'evil eye'?

Instead of letting fear disrupt your life, this book was written to show you how to harness its power. I'm inviting you to redefine fear, not as an obstacle but as a fire to fuel your forward momentum. Fear is not something to hide from but something to use as a guide, pushing you to seek more, learn more and grow more. I'm inviting you to feel the fear and rise above it, to stop worrying about what others think and instead focus on reaching further, exploring new places, connecting with new people and venturing into uncharted territories. Every time fear shows up, it's a signal that you're on the verge of unlocking a new part of yourself. By embracing fear and stepping through it, you'll uncover treasures within you that have yet to be activated. Redefining fear means knowing there is always more to discover, more to conquer. You'll use fear as your ally, and with every step you take beyond it, you'll prove it wrong, expanding your limits with each victory.

Fear constantly whispers, 'Hold on.'

It tells you, 'Wait until you lose the weight.' 'Wait until you have more money.' 'Wait until you're more experienced.' 'Wait until you have something to show.' 'Wait until tomorrow.' 'Wait until Monday.' But the question is, **how long will you keep waiting?** Hold on for what? For some perfect moment that doesn't exist?

Life is a conveyor belt moving at breakneck speed, always inviting you to jump on, to leap into your potential, to grab what's waiting for you. Life says, 'Come on, don't miss this! This moment is yours. Your greatness is here, right now!' but every time you say, 'Hold on,' you're turning life away. You're telling it, 'Not yet.' You're choosing to stay stuck in the waiting room, believing you're not ready.

The truth is, life is already happening right now, and if you're not where you want to be, it's because you've made a promise to yourself that you're not ready to jump in, but life doesn't wait. So, when will you stop holding on and start living the life that's rushing towards you?

Your secret is that you're waiting for the moment when you're finally fearless, but here's mine: you jump in with fear.

You don't need to be 'ready'. You don't need to have it all figured out. You just need courage. So, step into the unknown. Do something that makes your heart race. Do something that triggers your insecurities. Do something that scares the hell out of you because in those moments of fear, when you rise above it, something will shift. You will re-identify with yourself, not as the person who was once held back but as someone far stronger, more confident and more capable than you ever thought you were. Fear doesn't disappear; you simply learn how to stand tall in its presence, and in doing so, you become someone who no longer waits for the perfect moment but creates it instead.

Fear has the power to make you extraordinarily beautiful, even if you're unsure of what you're doing. When you rise above it, you'll discover a version of yourself you never knew existed. Over time, fear will stop being your enemy, and it'll be something you constantly work with instead.

Just a quick note: If your dreams, aspirations, passions or goals don't scare you just a little, then you're not playing big enough with your life. There should be at least three butterflies in your stomach. If not, you're too comfortable, and nothing new can grow from that. True expansion comes when you risk, change and make choices that push you beyond your limits.

Facing fear can bring you the fearless life you want.

- If you're afraid of failure, you're holding onto a story about a future that hasn't even happened yet.

- If you're afraid to get hurt in your next relationship, you're imagining a future that doesn't exist.

- If you're afraid of rejection, you're living in a narrative about the future that you've created in your mind.

- If you're afraid something is impossible to reach, you're projecting a future that hasn't come to pass.

- If you're feeling fearful, it's a sign that your belief system is misaligned with your true, limitless self.

Some of your most powerful lessons will be hidden in the thorns of pain, delivered through heartbreaks you feared, grief, setbacks, redundancies or even the hardest of life's circumstances, but you must train your mind to always seek the silver lining because that is where your true expansion lies.

You must always pay attention to where you stand in relation to what you're asking for. Saying, 'I want this,' is only part of the equation. Too often, you follow it up with, 'But this is where I am.' That 'but' creates an equal and opposite force to your desire. Imagine it like placing a powerful engine that pushes in one direction and another equal engine pushing in the opposite direction on a conveyor belt — what happens? The forces will cancel each other out, and no movement will occur. That is exactly why you feel stuck. As long as you hold two conflicting beliefs — desiring something while simultaneously affirming where you currently are — you'll remain at a standstill, unable to turn your thoughts into reality.

The next time you say, 'I want this,' don't stop there. Keep adding layer upon layer of positive beliefs, emotions and intentions until your desire has enough force to move through any resistance. Each positive thought you add is like another engine pushing your desire forward. Don't allow any engines of fear or doubt to move in the opposite direction because those will cancel out your progress. Keep loading your belief system with empowering thoughts, and soon you'll have the momentum needed to manifest your desire. If your dreams haven't shown up yet, it's because you've been adding engines of resistance instead—fear, doubt and hesitation—rather than fuelling them with unshakable faith and positivity.

It's absolutely crucial that you start being kinder to yourself if you want to live the life you've dreamt of. You have the power to transform every moment into something vibrant, so brighten up, energise yourself and bounce back stronger with every challenge. Take any feelings of disappointment, anger or frustration and turn them into joy, excitement, and enthusiasm. Remember, life is simply an energetic flow, and you control the current.

INTEGRATION

1. Write down 10 things you've been afraid to do. When was the last time you allowed yourself to step into them? Next to each item, write a date. Now, go and make it happen.

2. Be brutally honest with yourself: Which friends truly believe in you and your abilities? Which ones don't? Are you afraid to face their true opinion of you, and if so, why?

3. Write down three things you would do if you knew you couldn't fail. What would you dare to pursue if failure wasn't an option?

You Can Let Go Of Your Capitalist Desires

'Take a step back and realize [sic] most things are distractions.'

Maxime Lagacé

There are two types of desires.

Capitalist Desire: This is a desire rooted in the external world, a longing for material things, objects or experiences that are visible and tangible, often with the belief that these acquisitions will bring emotional or mental fulfilment.

Divine Quantum Desire: This is a longing for the Eternal, the infinite source that transcends time, space and physical form. It is an inner call to connect with something far beyond the limitations of the material world. It drives the pursuit of higher consciousness through practices like prayer, meditation and surrender.

Lust for capitalist desires can become a destructive force in your life because the constant craving for material things fuels the illusion that you are always lacking something. I'm not suggesting that you shouldn't want anything, but it's crucial to become hyper-aware of where you place your attention. If you remain unaware of where your focus lies, you can unwittingly perpetuate a cycle of scarcity and lack. The key is to recognise that desire doesn't have to be attached to your sense of self. In fact, when you detach from it, you free yourself from the grip it has on your happiness.

Letting go of your desires creates space for them to come to you in the most natural, effortless way. Picture it like a rubber band: When you pull it back, you accumulate energy, building momentum towards what you want. You hold that energy in the tension, picturing exactly what you desire, but the rubber band can't release the energy until you let go. Similarly, your desires need to be released in order to manifest. The moment you surrender them, the universe can guide them to you in the best possible way, far beyond what you could have imagined. Let go and trust that the perfect outcome will find you.

As human beings, we all experience obsessive thoughts, feelings and desires—it's part of our nature, and that's okay. The key isn't to push them away or try to fight them because doing so will only bring them back, sometimes even stronger. Anything you resist will simply return because there is no external place to push things away from. The only place these thoughts and feelings exist is within you. Instead of resisting, choose to focus on what you prefer, no matter how many times that obsessive thought or desire creeps in. Over time, your focus will shift, and that old pattern will fade away. The moment you stop trying to suppress or fight against what you don't want, you'll free yourself to embrace what you do want.

So, when that thought tells you to chase after something external, something artificial, you don't have to buy into it. The power is always with you to choose, to redirect your attention, to align with your true desires. You can welcome all thoughts and feelings without attachment, knowing you have the power to decide where you place your energy.

Dr David Hawkins' *Scale of Consciousness*[13] provides a framework for understanding our emotional and mental states, assigning numerical values to various levels of consciousness. At the highest end of the scale is *enlightenment* at 1,000, while at the lowest end is *shame* at 20. This scale essentially helps you rank your current state based on your thoughts, emotions and behaviours. It's a tool for deep self-reflection, allowing you to observe where you are energetically in any given moment.

Desire lands at a relatively low frequency of 125 on this scale, and while it might seem counterintuitive, the reason for this is simple: when you constantly desire things to be different—whether it's your life circumstances, your relationships or your self-image—you create an ongoing

---

13 Ferreira, E. (2023, March 6). Understanding Dr. David Haw-kins' Scale of Consciousness. Medium. https://medium.com/@edi. ferreira.net/understanding-dr-david-hawkins-scale-of-con-sciousness-da1bf8467b40

state of *lack*. The very act of desiring something else means you're living in a state of dissatisfaction, perpetuating feelings of yearning and inadequacy.

When we live in a state where we *want* things to be different, we inadvertently deepen our experience of pain and suffering. Desire pulls us out of the present moment and into a future that feels unattainable, simultaneously creating disconnection from the richness of what we already have. This is why, on the Scale of Consciousness, desire is considered a relatively low vibrational state—it keeps us stuck in a cycle of lack and prevents us from experiencing the peace and fulfilment that can only arise from acceptance and presence.

Change begins when you make the conscious choice to live abundantly in your mind, not just in response to the external world's limited definitions of what is possible. The ego often feeds on desires driven by outward validation and material pursuits, but real transformation happens when you transcend these surface-level cravings.

Throughout this journey, you must remember that desire is not inherently negative. Even with spiritual awakenings, we continue to feel the pull of desire. It may show up as a yearning to improve, to become kinder, to take inspired action or to experience more joy. Desire itself is not the problem; it's how we engage with it.

Inspiration flows towards you when your mind and heart are in tune. If what you're doing doesn't bring you joy, you're misaligned, and your desires won't come to pass as easily, but when you shift into service, your desires manifest quickly. Contrary to belief, service isn't sacrifice; it's the highest expression of your true self. Operating from love and heart-centred action creates a flow that brings everything you desire. The universe is held together by love, and when you give from the heart, everything comes to you with ease.

We live in a capitalist society that floods us with the desire for material luxuries, teaching us to race towards the grave with the shiniest toys. Capitalism conditions us to want more goods, not to seek inner growth or emotional wellbeing. It has robbed us of the chance to truly understand ourselves through self-expression and abundance. Instead, we are held hostage by philosophies that prioritise possessions over personal evolution, reinforcing the false belief that we are defined by what we acquire, not by who we become.

Divine quantum desire is not about striving to attain but allowing what is meant to be. The real breakthrough comes when you realise that by raising your consciousness — through self-acceptance, appreciation, love and honour — everything you seek will naturally follow.

It's time to live with detachment. Someone broke up with you? Detach. You didn't get the job? Detach. You're in overdraft? Detach. You feel lonely? Detach. The moment you stop resisting what is, you create space for better things to come.

You are bigger than all your desires. Put yourself on a pedestal and not your desires!

INTEGRATION

1. Throw out five items from your belongings. Either toss them or pass them on to someone who will appreciate them.

2. Identify five material desires you have, and for each one, write down the reason behind the craving and the reward you believe you'll get from having it.

3. Write down five ways you will ensure that no material possession will become the focal point of your life.

You Can Be Unreactive

'The principle is that any time you, as it were, you voluntarily let up control, in other words cease to cling to yourself, you have an excess of power. Because you're wasting energy all the time in self-defence. Trying to manage things, trying to force things to conform to your will. The moment you stop doing that, that wasted energy is available. In that sense, having the energy available you are one with the divine principle. You have the energy.'

Alan Watts

The greatest compliment I've ever received is when someone has told me they can *feel* my passion. It's not just a word or a brief sentiment; it's the fire that fuels every action, every thought, every ounce of energy I put into the world. When someone says they can feel it, it means that, for a moment, they've connected with the very core of what drives them. It's as though the invisible force that propels me forward has made its presence known to them, and in that recognition, I know I've touched something deeper than mere words or surface-level interaction.

We've all heard the common advice: 'Follow your passion,' or 'Never give up on your passion,' but passion isn't something to merely pursue or hold tightly on to. It's not an object you can possess; it's a living and breathing essence within you. It's a reminder that the most powerful forces in life are often the ones we cannot control but only surrender to.

The word 'passion' has evolved intensely over time. Its Latin root, *passio*, originally meant 'to suffer, endure or resign.' In the primaeval world, passion was often associated with pain, sacrifice and submission, but as the centuries passed, the meaning of the word underwent a weighty transformation.

During the Renaissance, a period of profound intellectual, artistic and cultural growth, passion began to take on a new life. It became a symbol of vibrant energy, inspiration and motivation, an awakening of the creative spirit. William Shakespeare, in his timeless works, spun the concept further, using passion to describe an intense, almost uncontrollable desire, particularly in romance. By the seventies, phrases like 'follow your passion' became mantras for a new generation, with Gen X and Millennials adopting it as an affirmation for personal fulfilment, pursuing what ignites their soul and chasing after their deepest desires with fervour and infatuation.

Passion is rich — *so* rich — in emotion and so thick with feeling. It's the one thing you can chase like it's the last bus of the night, desperate to catch it before it slips away. It's the thing that makes you feel *alive*, that makes your pulse quicken, your heart race and your spirit soar. Passion is an exhilarating surge of euphoria, a rush of *oomph* that propels you forward, no matter the obstacles, and irrefutably, no one — not a single soul — can take it from you.

I have many passions, but I have one that stands above them all, and it's one that truly drives me: to be in a constant and authentic relationship with myself. This isn't just a passing feeling for me; it's a deep, abiding passion. My happiness must be unconditional in order for me to stay in full alignment with this passion. It's the foundation of my entire sense of self, so if I find myself more miserable than joyful, more dissatisfied than content or more irritated than ecstatic, I know something's out of balance. It means I've allowed the external world — circumstances, people, situations — to cloud and distort the purity of myself. In those moments, my connection to this deep passion of authentic, unconditional happiness has been compromised. It's a constant reminder that my joy, my alignment and my peace cannot be dictated by the outside world — they must come from within. This is the standard I hold myself to. Anything less, and I know it's time to reset, recalibrate and return to the source of my truest passion.

I realised that if I truly want to step into the role of 'creator' in my own life, my happiness and resilience must be unconditional, no matter the circumstance. When we base our thoughts on conditions, we limit ourselves. Conditional thinking means you only entertain a thought long enough for it to manifest into something tangible, something you can touch or see or feel. Conditional thoughts are transactional by nature — they exist only for the return they promise: 'If I don't have this, I can't be happy.' But true emotional mastery lies in transcending this pattern. When you continuously and consciously choose to energise your happiness in every circumstance regardless of what's happening around you, it becomes more than a short-lived emotion—it becomes an intrinsic part of who you are. In doing so, you begin to naturally align with happiness, making it easier to find joy even in challenging situations.

To be unconditional in your thoughts means being willing to feel for the sake of feeling itself, not for any external transaction or to achieve a desired outcome, whether good or bad, but simply to embrace the experience of emotion as it arises. When you live this way, your happiness is no longer controlled by external conditions. To feel unconditionally happy, successful and enthusiastic means to also cultivate a sense of inner peace that will remain untouched by the world and its fluctuations. It means becoming unreactive to the people, situations or challenges that once triggered you. Over time, those who used to push your buttons or rattle your cage will notice a subtle shift that you no longer react, and as your reactivity diminishes, you'll find that the world begins to reflect this change back to you. More and more, you'll find yourself encountering circumstances that support your peace, enabling you to respond with ease. The more you embody this unshakable inner alignment, the more your outer world will mirror that same calm.

To be unconditional means to be appreciative no matter what, happy no matter what, graceful no matter what, kinder no matter what and loving no matter what. When you become rich in the beauty of your present life, no circumstance or person can pull you away from your natural state of peace and contentment.

Let's dive into a real-life example.

The money that flows into your life is not just currency—it's the direct, energetic exchange between you and the quantum field. The *key*—which shouldn't even be a secret—is learning to *remain unshaken* and *unreactive* by the conditions of your reality, no matter what your current bank balance reflects.

So many of you live surrounded by an abundance of love, knowledge, books, friendships, alcohol, clothes and joy, yet still struggle to attract the financial wealth you desire. Why does this happen? Because somewhere along the way, you've practised and fed the energy of *lack*. You've reacted more to the thought of not having enough money than having enough money. You've reacted more to the belief in not having enough more than your passions. You've reacted to the idea of scarcity instead of the certainty of abundance and the universe, with its perfect pair of ears, has listened to your energetic state and delivered your command.

Think about it: if your mind is constantly fixated on *not* having enough to pay your bills, if you define your financial worth only by the numbers on your monthly pay cheque if every decision is filtered through the lens of 'How much do I have right now?' or 'Maybe I can afford it next month if I miss out on this or that,' what energy do you really put into the world?

Consider every exchange you're making, every thought, every reaction, every energetic transaction. You can become so fixated on the *current* manifestation of money in your life that you forget the crucial truth: reacting to it only perpetuates more of what's already showing up. The more you engage with the reality of your finances from a place of scarcity, worry or frustration, the more that exact reality will keep repeating itself.

Putting your focus back on energy means embodying *richness* in every sense of the word long before it shows up in your bank account. Be *enthusiastically* rich in vitality, in your health, in your happiness, in your joy, in your laughter, in your generosity and in your capacity to receive. Be rich in the admiration of others, rich in your ability to give and rich in the full, expansive experience of life as it is right now. Romanticise the feeling of being *serene*, unshakable, nonchalant and powerful beyond all reason. Picture yourself fully aligned with a sense of abundance, not tied to circumstances or the current state of your finances. When you reach that state of being, when you *embody* that energy, regardless of what your bank balance looks like, the state of money must inevitably match your vibration.

One day, out of nowhere, a thought will spark within you or you'll cross paths with someone who presents an unexpected opportunity, an opening that you couldn't have planned for but that *aligns perfectly* with your energy. Why? Because you've reacted with something far greater than your current circumstances. You've shifted your vibration to a place where *miracles* can happen.

What you don't realise is that you're doing the *opposite* of what you need to do. You're matching your vibration to the state of your money because you live through your senses, looking at it, complaining about it, worrying over it and measuring it. If you can't see a huge pile of money, it's because you're not vibrationally ready for it. If you were truly aligned with abundance, you'd see it already.

Abundance will meet you as far as you are willing to meet it. If you can't see it, you haven't yet willed yourself to meet it.

There is infinite abundance all around you, waiting for you to ask for it, feel it and claim it. Just because it shows up for others doesn't mean it's less available for you. If you feel like abundance is 'running out' because others receive it, it's because you haven't yet fully willed yourself to align with the full potential of abundance. Stop being jealous of others because that emotion is rooted in scarcity. Jealousy is an indication that you're operating from a place of lack, believing that someone else's success or abundance somehow takes away from your own.

Being ready for money means being rich *without* it; it's as simple as that. You've got to be grateful for the sunshine, the rain, the clouds, your rusty old car, the chance to give someone else an opportunity, the strangers you meet, the chair you sit in, the warmth, the cold, every conversation. Be thankful for all the exchanges in your life. When your state of reaction is one of gratitude, everything in your life will begin to multiply. When you live in gratitude, the universe responds by giving you more to be grateful for.

I no longer view life through material possessions or by how others have attained what they have. Instead, I see life through energy and how rich in feeling someone must become to receive such things.

DEFINITIONS

The way you define or react to anything shows there is a part of your consciousness that agrees with what you react to, allowing you to perceive it in that way. You won't take anything personally if you understand it has nothing to do with you. You'll only feel affected by it if you subconsciously believe it to be true, if it resonates with some hidden belief you hold. Your reactions are a reflection of your own inner alignment, not the external world.

If you weren't wearing a necklace and someone came up to you and said, 'I hate your necklace,' you'd immediately recognise that their opinion had nothing to do with you. You wouldn't form a mental or emotional reaction because you'd know the statement was irrelevant. This shows that when you *do* react mentally or emotionally to something, it's because a part of you believes it to be true about yourself. If it didn't resonate with you in some way, you'd simply observe it and move on. Your reactions reveal where your inner alignment is and how much you are still holding onto certain beliefs about yourself.

When you become aware of why you've reacted the way you have, you'll gain clarity on where you need to nurture and heal, but if you don't uncover the 'why' behind your reactions, it will be much harder to move past them. It's always about the *why;* find your *whys.*

237

You cannot react with dissatisfaction and expect to attract what you want. Your dissatisfaction is a clear signal you're not vibrationally aligned with your desires. Greatness can only flow to a place *in sync* with greatness. To match that vibration, you must choose to think, feel and react positively, no matter the external circumstances. And the best part? It's not as difficult as you've made it out to be. To welcome greatness into your life, you must stop reacting to what isn't working, what you don't want, or what could have been.

We can choose to react with joy just as easily as we can react with negativity. Fixating on negative definitions is a choice, not a fate. When one door closes, eight more can open—*if* you choose to see them. The power is in your hands. How you respond to life's challenges is what determines the abundance of opportunities that follow.

INTEGRATION

1. Identify five situations that typically trigger a negative reaction in you.

2. For each situation, reflect on *why* you react the way you do and how you can respond differently the next time it arises.

3. List five practices or things that nurture your ability to react positively. How can you make these a consistent part of your week?

You Can Tune To Authenticity

'Be yourself so that everything and everyone looking for you can find you.'

Arlan Hamilton

There is nothing you *need* to do except fulfil your sacred purpose of being unapologetically and authentically *you*. That's it. That's the essence of life. The most exhausting journey you can take is the one where you try to be someone you're not, where you wear a mask and deform yourself to fit into a world that doesn't understand your rareness, but the most liberating and exhilarating journey you'll ever experience is the one where you stand *fully* in your truth, where you are completely, utterly and absolutely yourself.

Just as many of you have a signature scent in this day and age — one that perfectly captures your essence and personal preference — you also carry within you an unmistakable, authentic vibration. This vibration is a frequency that only you possess, a unique energy that cannot be bought, replicated, or faked. It cannot be found in any marketplace, nor can it be duplicated by others. It is yours, and only yours, to tap into and express fully.

For centuries, fears have been seeded into the very core of you — woven through the fabric of society, culture, and upbringing. These fears have planted subtle but powerful definitions of diminishment, devaluation, and disconnection, causing you dim your authenticity. Many of you have unknowingly allowed these fears to dim your light, to hold you back from expressing yourselves as fully as you are capable of.

Tuning to authenticity means aligning with your true self and acting on your highest excitement at every opportunity. If you can't always do this, then pursue your highest excitement as much as you can. Being authentic is about embracing your individuality with nerve and expressing what matters most to you, not in doubt or hesitation but with confidence, fearlessness, adventure and passion.

Authenticity is about tapping into your creativity, imagination and vision and allowing them to guide you, not your friends' or your family's authenticity, *no*, your own.

It's also about not holding back the unique offerings and gifts you are meant to give and not depriving others of the opportunities and blessings that only *you* can provide. While you may feel like you're on a journey to discover your own path, remember that others—just like you—are searching for the very things only you are destined to share, give and deliver to them. Authenticity is not just about your own growth but about empowering others to thrive and succeed just as you do. Your true purpose is realised when you uplift both yourself and those around you.

When you stand in a state of deep knowing, feeling, and reacting from the truth that your life—exactly as it is right now—is as perfect as it can be, you will have mastered your authenticity. When you embrace your authentic self and recognise that nothing needs to change in this moment, that everything is already in its rightful place, you will radiate a sense of power. This energy you cultivate within yourself will naturally extend to others, creating a ripple effect of authenticity. Not only will you embody your truest self, but you will also be a living testament to authenticity, inspiring and empowering those around you to do the same. When you are authentic, you show others that they, too, can be authentic.

Whatever shows up for you right now is *authentic* to you; it was always meant to happen, to reveal just how much further you are capable of going. Authenticity doesn't fight or resist what happens; it embraces everything with the understanding that every person and every experience that crosses your path has a purpose. Each encounter, whether challenging or uplifting, is meant to authenticate you even further, helping you refine and deepen your true self.

If you're feeling fear, depletion, devaluation and disconnection, it's a sign that these exhausting emotions are reflecting an inauthentic self, one that isn't fully aligned with your true capacity. These feelings indicate that you're not living in your fullest truth. If this resonates with you, know that now is the moment to take your first step towards embracing your true state.

So, now is the time to recognise that closed doors are not punishments; rejection is a gift, and waiting can be a powerful teacher. Let go of feelings of depletion, devaluation and disconnection and step into a space of happiness, knowing that this moment is just the beginning of your greatness. When you allow yourself to lead and follow the path of least resistance, embracing what is — no matter what's happened, no matter how you've spiralled or felt lost — those spirals will become your voyages. They will be the very journeys that help you discover more of who you truly are, what you authentically love, and what makes you feel truly alive. If these experiences weren't essential, they wouldn't exist, but they do, and they exist for one vital purpose: to help you understand your richness and the unique essence of yourself more clearly than ever before.

What I mean by tuning to authenticity is being fully present with everything you have become and everything you have lived and manifested. Your authenticity is made up of all your experiences — the pain, the struggle, the triumphs and the lessons. It's reflected in your past, your future opportunities and the cycles of beginnings and endings. Your authenticity is not just what you are in this moment but everything you have been, everything you are and everything you will ever be. It is your entire energy stream, from start to infinity. So, don't ever regret what has happened in your life because this is as authentic as it can get.

Even when the moment doesn't align with your preferences, your authenticity thrives when you choose to embrace it fully, allowing yourself to respond with love, power and unwavering presence. It's about feeling the sunshine even when there are clouds, rain and thunder and seeing the light even when it's dark, dim or dusky. You must be content with every step of your evolution—happy with the rain, happy with the money, happy with your home, happy with every part of your inner and outer world. You must find joy in every experience, embracing almost everything in your life with gratitude. When you're satisfied with each step of your growth, you'll celebrate every podium you stand on. If you can't find happiness on the smaller 'baby' podiums you're on now, you'll never be truly fulfilled by the greater milestones your life has yet to offer.

How do you know if you're *truly* being authentic?

It's very simple: you'll feel absolutely wonderful, absolutely gorgeous and absolutely amazing *right now*. The key is not demanding this feeling from yourself at every moment but being conscious of it as often as possible. When you allow yourself to be present with joy and positivity, you align with your true essence. However, if you consciously choose negative emotions, you'll distance yourself from your authentic self. By embracing the positive, you'll stay rooted in your true authenticity, creating space for more of it to flow into your life.

If you wish that the moment were different than it is, you're not being your authentic self. To truly know that everything is okay is to recognise that what's unfolding before you is exactly as it should be. Being authentic isn't about resisting or pushing away what life presents; it's about relaxing into it, trusting that every experience has a purpose. No matter what happens, the present moment gives you the clarity to better understand what you *do* want, and that insight fuels your authenticity moving forward. You begin to make every choice, reaction and thought aligned with your truest self, embracing life as it comes. So many of us wish for things to be different—better circumstances, more compassion, more passion, more effort. When we're caught in the cycle of wanting more than what we have right now, we become resistant to receiving anything at all.

When you are authentic, you won't be swayed by what others think, say or believe about you. This is because when you are living as your true self, you won't attract anything that contradicts it. If you find yourself uncertain in your power and someone's perception of you causes you to feel diminished, take that moment to remind yourself that your path is about *you*, not them. Your authenticity is not dependent on others; it is entirely about your own alignment. When you stay true to your authentic self, the opinions of others will no longer have the power to shake you but align and mirror you.

When your consciousness rises, you'll realise that all your adversities were never truly outside of you but always reflections of what was out of alignment with your own authenticity.

INTEGRATION

1. Identify five authentic personality traits you've always kept hidden, fearing judgement from others. Now, give yourself permission to express them openly, starting today.

2. Write down five things you do in private that you wish you could share with the world. What's stopping you from expressing them?

3. Make three powerful promises to yourself that will nurture and honour your authenticity moving forward.

You Can Flow

'Seek not that the things which happen should happen as you wish; but wish the things which happen to be as they are, and you will have a tranquil flow of life.'

Epictetus

Your mind is the catalyst; everything else flows from it.

When you actively seek signs in your outer world rather than allow them to flow naturally, you energetically signal to the quantum field that you lack faith. If you truly trusted that your desires were already on their way, you wouldn't feel the need to search for signs. When negative thoughts arise, you don't go looking for signs that they will manifest, so why do you do this with the things you want? It's crucial to examine the beliefs and emotions driving your actions of inadequacy because they reveal the hidden blocks within you that prevent anything from flowing effortlessly.

You will never see a sign of something before you impress it upon your subconscious mind and consciously ask for it. The signs don't pave the way for the manifestation. Rather, the manifestation is already set in motion and will always succeed unless you doubt it. The signs simply follow your thoughts like an echo.

When Neville Goddard said, 'The signs always follow. They do not precede,'[14] he meant that as you begin to shift your self-concept, elevate your frequency and move

---

14 Quoted in Spencer, K. (2023, September 7). Signs always follow. They never precede. Medium. https://medium.com/punchy-lite-bites/signs-always-follow-they-never-precede-822b52c0c41e

into alignment with your desires, synchronicities and coincidences naturally unfold. These signs are simply reflections of the inner transformation you've already initiated.

When you doubt yourself, you're not fully aligned with your natural flow — do you understand what doubt really is?

Doubt is simply 100% trust in a reality you don't prefer, so why not shift that trust to something you *do* prefer since you're already trusting in something anyway? There's no such thing as a lack of trust — doubt is just trust in the wrong thing. You must trust in something, or you won't have any experience at all. The key isn't learning how to trust; it's becoming aware of where you're placing your trust, and since the universe has already shown you that trusting in what you don't want has brought you these experiences, why not assume that trusting in what you *do* want will bring just as much, if not more, support?

When you're impatient, you're also out of sync with your natural flow — do you understand what patience *really* is?

The only reason we might feel we need patience is because we experience impatience. If you're doing what you love in every moment, what do you need patience for? When you truly understand the nature and structure of your existence, you begin to see that many concepts are misunderstood. Patience is often thought of as the ability to wait calmly for something to happen, but in reality, it's more about being in perfect balance with what's already unfolding.

Living in the present moment means accepting and allowing everything as it is without hurry or resistance. The key difference is that when you're fully engaged in the moment, you enjoy it deeply, no matter what's happening. You don't *need* patience because you're not waiting for something better to come along. The moment you're in is already enough. So, when you're immersed in the present, there's no need for patience because impatience doesn't exist—you don't wish to be anywhere other than where you are. Patience isn't a part of the equation because you're already aligned with the flow of life.

You disempower the flow of your life when you place more importance on external signs, like angel numbers, a feather that randomly appears, a butterfly landing on your nose or a crystal you believe holds your entire energetic life force. The issue is that by focusing so much on these outside symbols, you divert your attention from the true power within you. When we prioritise external signs, we overlook the incredible creative potential we already hold inside. This causes us to worry more about finding validation from the outside world instead of trusting the guidance and power within ourselves.

It's time to learn how to flow with the rhythm of this beautiful life. If you ever find yourself in doubt and searching for signs, take a moment to pause and ask yourself these questions:

- Am I seeking signs because I don't trust myself enough?

- Why do I feel the need for validation from 11:11 or other external cues?

- Am I searching for signs because I don't fully embody the feeling of the wish fulfilled?

Trust the flow of life, surrender to its natural rhythm and have faith in the divine intelligence that governs all things, an intelligence far greater than the limitations of our human minds.

INTEGRATION

1. List five areas where you feel confident in your lack.

2. List 10 areas where you feel confident in abundance.

3. Write down five new, positive, affirmative beliefs that will help you flow into greater abundance. Read them every day for a week.

You Can Move Mountains

'There are dandelions growing through cracks in the sidewalk. There is a fence lizard on the porch who is growing a new tail. There are trees growing through an abandoned house, branches tearing through the ceiling, ferns carpeting the floor. There is life pushing forward, pushing through.'

Unknown

Empowerment isn't about waiting for confirmation—it's about believing and feeling it within yourself, always and without question. To be empowered is to be fully free from the judgements and opinions of others, knowing they can never understand the entire context of everything you've done and will do in your life simply because they are not you.

When we see someone else's success, we often feel compelled to mirror them, trying to mould ourselves to replicate their exact path. We attempt to shape ourselves to fit someone else's truth, but the truth society has long overlooked is that true empowerment comes from embracing your own authenticity. Nobody will ever do what you do, deliver what you deliver, speak how you speak, or be you in the way you are. We must learn to celebrate others' successes while also honouring the fact that no one can do you better than you, just as no one can do them better than they can. When we forget there is limitless abundance for all, we sometimes hold back from giving others the recognition they deserve. Empowerment means allowing both yourself and others to be fully authentic, even if their journey is ahead of yours. Always choose truth over judgement and encourage others to do the same.

Empowerment isn't defined by where you are but by who you are in that moment, regardless of external circumstances. It's never about what happens outside of you but about how you *respond* to what happens outside of you. This is the true measure of empowerment. Your happiness has always been an inside job; it's never been dependent on an external reflection. Only you have the power to decide your state of being, and the outer world will eventually mirror that inner state. The truest form of empowerment does not need that reflection to change because you no longer base your worth or happiness on it. If you do, then your sense of empowerment becomes conditional.

There will be many moments when people won't agree with who you are or the message you share simply because you are fully empowered in your own truth. When you show up as *you*—in your most authentic, unapologetic form—you become a mirror for others who aren't yet being their true selves. Sometimes, people won't like that reflection, but this is the greatest act of love and service you can offer to anyone. By simply being yourself, you give others the opportunity to see that they, too, can be empowered and authentic whether or not they choose to take it.

By not stepping into your full authenticity, you deny others the chance to see that they can live more freely, more powerfully and truer to who they are. You allow their fears and egos to stay in control, but when you choose to be unapologetically *you*, you become a force, an example for others to follow. You give them a chance to think, 'If it's working for them maybe I can do it, too.'

In doing so, you don't just expand yourself—you become an expander for others, offering them new possibilities. You invite them to break free from their own fears and limitations, showing them that the path to authenticity is open and waiting. In doing this, you create a ripple effect of empowerment and abundance because you do not hoard your truth; you share it. This is what the world truly needs: more people living fully, freely and authentically. By suppressing your authenticity, you inadvertently reinforce the belief that fear and disempowerment are acceptable, but when you stand fully in your truth, you empower others to do the same.

To be truly empowered is to embrace the present moment, fully accepting that exactly where you are right now is where you are meant to be. It's not about meeting the expectations of others or following the path you think you should be on, but about trusting that what is unfolding in your life right now is exactly what you need. Empowerment doesn't come from seeing, touching or hearing something external that confirms you are where you need to be. That's conditional living, tied to external validation. When you expect things to show up in a specific way, you limit your potential because you're boxing yourself into a narrow vision of what's possible. This expectation closes you off to the limitless opportunities and abundance that could be right in front of you. Empowerment means you keep your focus open, knowing that even if things don't show up the way you *thought* they would, your confidence, excitement and positivity remain unshaken. If your state of being fluctuates because your desires haven't materialised as expected, it's a sign that you haven't yet transformed at a deeper level. Why should your reality change if you haven't yet changed either? To truly empower yourself, it must become a way of life, unwavering no matter the circumstances.

Self-authenticity is the core of true empowerment. When the self isn't aligned—when it isn't happy, confident, connected or flowing—it cannot experience true power. Instead, it becomes fearful of being all that it truly is. Fear-based beliefs are learnt and adopted from external sources, and they limit us from expressing our authentic selves. If we're not born with these fear-based systems, then they don't belong to us, and they were passed on to us by others. Empowerment means releasing these inherited beliefs because you recognise that you're better off without them. When the self is authentic, it knows no fear. If fear arises, it means the self has been distorted by something external.

It's crucial to recognise when you carry beliefs that aren't your own. If you find yourself stuck in a negative cycle because the external world doesn't reflect what you want, it's time to identify the belief systems holding you back from your authentic power. Once your conscious mind discovers a fear-based belief, you'll realise how illogical and irrational it truly is. However, if you continue to hold onto it, it means there is another underlying belief that makes the first one seem valid. This is where the real work lies. You must continue to dig deeper into your belief systems, uncovering the root belief that holds everything else in place. Once you see this belief for what it is—irrational and unfounded—you'll be able to release the entire web of limiting beliefs, freeing yourself to step into your authentic power.

You'll know you've not uncovered the ringleading belief when you notice that despite your efforts, you keep thinking, feeling, behaving and experiencing the same patterns over and over again. If you find yourself stuck in repetitive cycles, it's a clear sign you haven't yet identified the core belief that's driving them. The ringleading belief is the one that, once recognised and released, dissolves all the smaller, limiting beliefs tied to it. Until that happens, the cycle persists.

Empowerment starts with recognising the potential in every small seed, even when the bigger picture doesn't unfold as expected. Do you have access to clean, consistent water? There are many millions of people who don't share that same certainty. Wake up to the abundance around you. When you shift into a conscious state of gratitude in every moment, you'll soon realise it's life's most powerful multiplier. Gratitude doesn't just shift your mindset—it transforms your reality.

Visualisation is a powerful tool to help you envision the life you desire, but in an age where material manifestation is so heavily emphasised, it can unintentionally disempower you. The purpose of visualisation isn't to force a specific outcome but to create a metaphorical representation of an ideal scenario that excites you about what's possible. Your physical mind can't comprehend the full extent of your ideal outcome, so it's essential to train your mind to acknowledge that you don't know exactly what your ideal outcome is. By doing this, you open yourself up to receiving something far greater than what you've pictured. When you cling too tightly to a specific result, you limit the potential for something even more extraordinary to manifest. The last thing you want is to block your own path with rigid expectations.

Inward empowerment means that nothing—neither what happens nor what doesn't—can shake your inner strength. It doesn't matter how things look, feel or sound on the outside because you trust that everything is always happening for your ultimate benefit. If you instilled the belief system that everything ever happens to benefit you, you wouldn't care what happens.

Imagine the immense power of not needing clothes to define your worth, makeup to enhance your beauty, shoes to symbolise your success or diamonds to feel seen. Your true power lies within, and once you harness it, you'll become the light that illuminates your world.

INTEGRATION

1. Reflect on five moments where your resilience shone through in the past.

2. Write down five powerful words of encouragement you've received from others that uplifted you. Repeat these affirmations to yourself throughout this week.

3. Take the time to reflect on three key areas of your life where you can elevate your personal power and strength.

You Can Speak Life

'Do not feel lonely, the entire universe is inside you. Stop acting so small. You are the universe in ecstatic motion. Set your life on fire.'

Rumi

If you change your words, you can change your world.

Your language reinforces your beliefs and defines how you see yourself. It's a powerful tool that can shift your focus away from perceived failures and draw you closer to your inherent strengths. Words carry immense power—this is why we often hear people say you can 'speak things into existence'. Why? Because words trigger emotions, and those emotions act as a magnetic force, attracting experiences and people that align with your inner state.

Speaking life isn't just about changing your external dialogue; it's about transforming your inner dialogue as well. It's one of the foundational pillars that lead you towards your truth. If you can master everything in the *You Can Series* but miss this, you're simply setting yourself up for another lesson.

Speaking life is like paracetamol but for the soul, how you speak to yourself, how you support and believe in yourself. Life is too short to let opportunities slip by because of the dim and limiting conversations you have within or with others. When you speak life, you empower yourself to rise above the noise, unlock your potential and invite a reality aligned with your highest self.

The words we use in both our inner and external dialogue has a profound impact on our emotions and moods. Consider this simple example: we all have opinions about the weather, and without fail, we express them regularly.

The science behind this is fascinating.

Language and emotions are deeply intertwined, operating in the same area of the brain. This connection means that the words you use can trigger a stress response, amplifying negative emotions. When you speak negatively about someone or something, you are not just describing it — you are fuelling your own emotional reaction, intensifying the very feelings you aim to avoid.

Consistently speaking negatively strengthens neural pathways linked to negative emotions, setting it as a default pattern for future thoughts. The mind is a powerful tool, capable of rewiring itself based on the thoughts and experiences you continually feed it. This means your habitual language shapes your mindset and emotional responses, creating a cycle that reinforces negativity unless consciously redirected.

Even more profoundly, negative language can trigger psychosomatic responses, where the mind directly influences the body. This means that negative descriptions, such as complaining about the weather, can amplify physical discomfort because your body reacts to the situation through the lens of your words. The mind and body are deeply interconnected, and the language you use can either ease or intensify the physical sensations you experience.

This also reinforces cognitive biases, meaning that negative language can shape how you remember and perceive events. For example, if you consistently associate rain and clouds with the word 'miserable', your mind will start to filter out other aspects of the experience and focus only on the negative. As a result, whenever you encounter similar weather conditions in the future, you'll automatically perceive them as miserable, reinforcing the same pattern of thought and emotional response.

I'm encouraging you to see that, even in the presence of rain, thunder and dark clouds, you have the power to choose how you feel. You can decide to embrace the cleansing, calming or cosy qualities these moments bring. The words you use to describe the weather — or anything in life — are merely labels you've assigned to them. Ultimately, life is all about your perception. Whatever conditions arise, you have the ability to choose how you respond to them, shaping your reality with your thoughts and feelings.

In essence, by consciously choosing positive language and uplifting words, you have the power to reshape your mindset and elevate your emotional state no matter what's happening around you. This shift in perception enables you to see the diamonds in the dust, the silver linings and the breaks in the clouds simply because your mind is focused on solutions, not problems. When you change the way you speak, you change the way you experience life.

Words are better sweet than sour.

INTEGRATION

1. Write a heartfelt thank you letter to yourself, acknowledging a challenging experience you've successfully navigated. Recognise your strength, resilience and the lessons learnt through that process.

2. Throughout this week, pay close attention to any negative thoughts or affirmations that arise. Each time you notice one, immediately transform it into a positive affirmation. Commit to shifting your mindset each time you catch yourself thinking negatively.

3. Every day for a week, list three wins—big or small—that you've achieved. At the end of the week, make it a daily habit to reflect on your accomplishments, reinforcing your progress and cultivating gratitude.

You Can Create Greater Moments

'Don't leave before the miracle.'

Unknown

At the start of each day, you need to make the conscious decision to romanticise the hell out of every moment: your mornings, afternoons, evenings and everything else in between. You owe it to yourself to begin doing the things you once dreamed of before fear, doubt or worry crept in. Just one passing moment of bravery before the sun rises can set the tone for the entire day, sparking the belief that your dreams are actually within reach. Perhaps the path that terrifies you the most is the one you'll take when you consciously choose to make your mornings greater than they've ever been.

In a world often weighed down by heaviness and uncertainty, optimism can seem like a rare commodity, but maybe the collective remedy we need is to romanticise the life we have just a bit more, to embrace the idea that the miraculous is real and magic exists all around us. If we believe that miracles aren't real, we'll never accept them when they cross our paths. On the other hand, if we choose to believe in the unexpected, in serendipitous miracles, we'll start to see them everywhere.

Your decision to create meaningful moments throughout your day is a reflection of the respect you have for yourself. Until you fully honour and respect who you are, the way you show up in life—what you do, how you do it and when you do it—will always be limited. Self-respect is the willingness to alchemise your thoughts, feelings and actions on demand. It means taking full responsibility for your discomfort, for the soreness of breaking out of your old patterns and doing what it takes to live the life you've always dreamed of.

It's easy to fall into the familiar comfort of the same routine, the same predictable Mondays, because it feels safer, but if you truly want something different, you'll have to move differently. If you don't, then you never really wanted different in the first place.

If this resonates with you, let this be the moment you stop tolerating less than you deserve. There is simply no more time to waste on anything less than your truth. If you want to be understood, speak up and explain. If you're curious, ask questions. If you like something, share it. If you want something, make the request, and if someone says no, remember: **you're asking the wrong person**. If you don't want to do something, simply say no. If you love someone, tell them.

When people say, 'New year, new me,' I don't think they fully grasp its potential. The phrase often becomes a fleeting declaration— 'New year, new me' until the challenge feels too big, too distant or too difficult to sustain. Or, it's 'New year, new me' until the initial excitement fades, and by the time we hit March, we've completely forgotten what our resolutions were, but greater moments don't just happen on the first day of a new year; they unfold every single day. Each day holds the possibility for reinvention, for growth, for a shift that propels us forward. A true transformation isn't about waiting for the calendar to flip, *no*. It's about waking up every day and deciding: *Today, I'll move forward*. It's about building the momentum of your vision through passion, purpose and, above all, *reason*.

As a writer, passion is what pushes my pen to the paper, and I've come to realise that we never summon the enthusiasm needed to manifest a vision unless we first discover the *reason* behind it. That's the secret. It's the driving force that separates those who spend endless hours scrolling through social media, lost in the comfort of tomorrow's promises and those who choose to *act* today. It's the difference between those who say, 'Tomorrow, tomorrow,' and those who boldly say no to distractions, turning down invitations to the party because they're too busy unlearning the things they've been spoon-fed, knowing deep down that the old narratives no longer taste sweet.

Each greater moment should spark excitement, ignite motivation and inspire you to step beyond your comfort zone. In fact, it should even inject a little bit of fear into you because if you don't feel the slightest bit scared if you don't feel that edge of uncertainty, then you're playing it too safe, and when you play it safe, you'll never discover just how high you can truly fly.

There is no more time to make excuses. To create a life filled with greater moments, you must choose to want something greater, and you must choose it relentlessly. The greater option must become second nature to you. For instance, your parents did the best they could, but their choices hurt you—what will you choose to believe and heal from? You love someone, but you know keeping them in your life isn't healthy—what will you choose to prioritise, your peace or your attachment? You're terrified of taking the next step, but deep down, you know it's the right one—will you choose courage or stay stuck in your fear? You're afraid to fail, but you have faith in your own abilities—what will you choose to act on? You long for healthy relationships, but unresolved trauma makes it hard—will you choose healing, even when it's uncomfortable? There aren't enough hours in the day, but you spend much of it on autopilot—will you choose presence, choice and conscious action?

It's time to start your shift work now. Shift your wake time, your work time, your dinner time, your bedtime—your entire approach to daily life. Don't let your subconscious fool you into thinking you're not a morning person because if you truly want something, you'll make the change. Just like they say, 'If he wanted to, he would,' the same applies to you and your life.

MEDITATION

Meditation is a powerful gateway to greater moments. It offers you the opportunity to disconnect from every energetic bond you've formed with the outside world, severing ties with the people, places, times and circumstances that have shaped your reality. When you remove sensory input from your surroundings, your inner world becomes more real than the external one you've been conditioned to focus on. In that stillness, you reclaim your energy, drawing it back from the distractions that normally pull you in multiple directions. Each time you sit in meditation, you break free from the program you've been running, allowing yourself the freedom to step outside the limitations of your habitual thoughts, and with every break from the old patterns, new possibilities arise, leading your life in unexpected and transformative directions. Meditation isn't just a pause; it's the moment where you step into the power of your true potential.

Meditation is a realm of magic and shapeshifting, where the ordinary becomes extraordinary. In this sacred space, beds transform into boats and sheets unfurl as sails, guiding you across wild seas made of pillows. Tea towels morph into capes of invincibility, and colanders turn into astronauts' helmets, ready to launch you into the stars. It's a playground of the mind where the limits of reality are cast aside, and you are free to create a world you can call yours.

However, don't be fooled—meditation isn't just a practice you reserve for 10 to 30 minutes a day, no. It's a state of being, a quality, a way of life that you carry with you every waking moment. True transformation isn't about how long you sit in stillness; it's about how you think and feel *as long as your eyes are open*. Being meditative while you're awake means staying anchored in that state throughout your day. It's about not letting the material world dictate your focus. Instead, your attention remains on the infinite possibilities, the spontaneous opportunities and the miracles that await you at every turn. This state has the power to reduce anxiety and depression, increase your tolerance to pain and elevate your memory and self-awareness. The practice of silent sitting is essential to shifting your brainwaves from a state of survival back into creation, where new possibilities arise. The worst thing that could happen from meditation is that you get healthy—mentally, emotionally and spiritually.

If you rise from meditation feeling the same as when you first laid down, then the work isn't done yet. The goal is to persist until the tension in your body releases, the clenching of your jaw softens, your shoulders drop, your belly relaxes and, most importantly, your mind quiets.

- To create something infinite, you must embody and feel boundless.

- To create something beautiful, you must embody and feel beautiful.

- To create something extraordinary, you must embody and feel extraordinary.

- To create something joyous, you must embody and feel joy.

- If you find it hard to meditate, try incorporating these mindful practices into your daily life:

- Pause before each sip of coffee, feel the warmth and aroma grounding yourself in the present moment.

- Eat without electronic distractions, allowing yourself to fully experience the textures, tastes and sensations of your food.

- Simply say, 'Thank you' before every meal, cultivating gratitude in each bite.

- Sit in silence for 10 minutes, focusing on a single object, observing its details and allowing your mind to settle.

- Stop and listen to the sounds around you. Acknowledge each one as it comes and goes.

- Visualise the key you hold to unlock opportunities, potential and abundance with each turn.

- As you shower, imagine the water cleansing and releasing any negative energy or emotional weight you've carried.

- Infuse your morning coffee or tea with powerful intentions as you stir clockwise, feeling the energy flow into your day.

- Look at yourself in the mirror and affirm, 'Today is going to be a great day.'

- Focus on your breath, gently noticing the rise and fall of your chest with each inhale and exhale.

- Gaze at the sky and marvel at the vastness of the clouds, letting their movement bring you peace.

- Observe the details around you, how many strands of grass, leaves, or grains of sand are present. Take in the beauty of the infinite.

- While waiting in queues, pause to observe your surroundings, the texture of the walls, the light dancing through the windows, the rhythm of life unfolding.

AFFIRMATIONS

Abundance understands the potent power of affirmations because the words we say after 'I am' are deeply absorbed by the unconscious mind and shape our reality. Abundance knows that affirmations must be used with intention and consistency, like a rhythm that eventually becomes second nature — your new language. Words are like healing balms; just as they soak into and soothe the skin, they can also soak into your mind, bringing nourishment to the places within you that need it most. With each affirmation, you reprogramme your subconscious, aligning it with the truth of your abundant potential.

At some point in your life, you've been in a crowded room surrounded by chatter and noise, yet if someone calls your name, you hear it instantly as it cuts through the chaos. The reason this happens is because your brain has set a filter for your name, knowing it's one of the most significant words in your life. Affirmations work in the same way. When you repeat them with intention, they become like filters in your mind, tuning your focus to the opportunities and gateways that align with your affirmations. Just as you can't help but hear your name in a crowd, the world will begin to reveal the paths that resonate with your affirmations, making your intentions clearer and more accessible.

According to research, the average person thinks about 60,000 thoughts per day. Of those, approximately 75%—or 45,000—are negative, and a staggering 95% of them are repetitive. This makes affirmations incredibly powerful. By regularly practising them, either out loud or internally, you have the ability to rewire your mind. With consistent repetition, you can transform those 75% negative thoughts. Through this process, the repetitive nature of your thoughts can shift and eventually cultivate a deep belief in the positive affirmations you reinforce, allowing you to alchemise negativity into empowering, constructive thinking.

Once again, you must affirm without needing to know *how*, *what*, *why* or *when* something will happen. Trust in the process and surrender to the certainty that it will align for you in ways you could never have anticipated.

NATURE

If you could take just 10 minutes out of your day to lay on the soil, barefoot, with your palms facing the earth, listening to the soft whispers of the birds, you'd learn more than you could ever from reading 1,001 books. Nature is not only a mirror to your soul, but it is the most honest, unfiltered version of reality you can experience. The trees, the breeze, the quiet hum of life — it all speaks to you in ways words cannot. When you attune yourself to the rhythm of Nature, you reconnect with a truth that transcends time. In that space, you become one with the abundance of life and, in turn, one with the deepest answers to your questions. Nature doesn't lie; it simply *is*, and by immersing yourself in its simplicity, you unlock the purest form of understanding.

The next time you lie back and listen to Nature, you'll realise it's not just a series of random sounds but an intricate orchestra, a symphony of life in perfect harmony. It's a galaxy of language unfolding in whispers and vibrations you may have never noticed before. As you gaze at the shifting sky above, you might feel a moment of dizziness, a sense of wonder at how vast it all is, but if you surrender to the rhythm of it, if you let go into the underground world beneath you, you'll begin to grow with the trees, sway with the breeze, and flow with the water. In that moment, you'll realise that by mirroring the fluidity, patience and acceptance of Nature, nothing can be in resistance. You, too, will become part of the natural current, moving with ease and grace through every twist and turn of your life.

There is an endless well of abundance surrounding us, always right in front of our eyes, yet we often miss it until we learn to truly see it. When you feel like you don't have enough, take a moment to look outside your window and witness the vastness of the world that you are a part of. Start with the wind that swirls around you, the way it tousles your hair, or the countless litres of water resting deep in the ocean. Can you count how many blades of grass fill a park? How about the grains of sand on the shore? It's immeasurable, infinite. This is the kind of abundance we live with every single day, always there, always plentiful, always available. Once you shift your awareness, you'll realise that abundance is not just something we seek but something we're immersed in at all times.

I hope that, through Nature, you'll come to realise you never lack anything.

INTEGRATION

1. Take a peaceful 20-minute walk in nature, allowing yourself to fully immerse in the sights, sounds and sensations around you.

2. Fill your space with a scent that uplifts your spirit—whether it's candles, incense or a diffuser, let it be a reminder of comfort and calm.

3. Treat yourself to something special this week, one simple yet meaningful gift that brings you joy and nurtures your sense of self-love.

The 20 Rules to Being Human

Success, fulfilment and purpose in life are often shaped by the principles we choose to live by. While the journey is rarely without its obstacles, making intentional choices and aligning with the right priorities enables us to make the most of every moment. Like any game, the key to thriving through life's toughest challenges is having a clear strategy and staying true to what matters most.

1. Your physical reality mirrors your self-concept.

2. Transcend the limitations of your senses, body, environment and time.

3. The purpose of life is to serve and contribute.

4. Energy is neither created nor destroyed; it is constantly evolving and transforming.

5. You must consistently live, breathe and feel from a place of pure energy.

6. Reality is born from the imagination and thoughts of your mind.

7. Live in alignment with the fifth dimension—creation begins with the seed of your thoughts and emotions.

8. Master the power of mind over matter; life's adventure is to learn the art of alchemy.

9. Happiness is not a distant hope, it is a state of being.

10. Nothing is ever your fault, but everything is your responsibility.

11. Selfishness is, in truth, a form of selflessness.

12. We are all interconnected; separation is an illusion.

13. Abundance will meet you as far as you are willing to meet abundance—extend it to both your friends and enemies.

14. There is more than enough to go around for everyone.

15. Life happens for you; never to you as a victim.

16. You are not defined by your output or what you produce.

17. You don't need to achieve anything to be worthy—you already are.

18. Failure is merely a step forward on the path to success.

19. The greatest purpose you'll ever encounter is the exploration of the question, 'Who am I?'

20. Love is the answer to all things.

The Adventure of a Lifetime

Seven years, six months and 15 days ago, I walked away from everything I had ever known, hoping that in leaving behind the familiar, I could somehow find peace after my brother's passing. I didn't know what happiness looked like anymore. I didn't even know if I *believed* in it, but seven years, six months and 15 days later, I stand here, stronger, more whole and more at peace than I ever thought possible, not just with the world around me but with the person I've become.

It's a strange thing to realise. I used to count the days, tallying the hours as if grief could somehow be outrun, as if healing was a destination that could be reached if I just pushed myself hard enough, but the truth is my life, with all its peaks and valleys, has unfolded in the most unexpected ways. Life didn't wait for me to be ready. It didn't ask for my permission to move forward, and somewhere along the way, I stopped fighting that fact.

As much as it pains me to say it out loud, *life goes on*. And eventually, life did go on. I'm sorry, but how could it not? It took me a long time to accept that, and when I finally did, slowly and quietly, I came to understand something about myself: grief didn't just change me; I changed it. For so long, I felt like I was tethered to a moment in time, to a grief that felt as if it would swallow me whole, but somehow, life found a way to pull me through. I found a way to walk with it, to carry it forward, not as a burden but as a reminder of my strength and my resilience.

Every time I look into the mirror, I see her, the version of myself who didn't know how to go on. She's still there in the lines of my face, in the quiet spaces between my thoughts, but I no longer try to push her away. Instead, I bring her flowers. I tell her, *I will keep you alive by showing you the beauty that exists on the other side of this pain.*

I remember a time when I looked at photos of myself as a child: tiny hands, chubby legs, and that smile that could light up the world. I promised that little girl I would do better for her, that I would take this life and turn it into something mesmerising. I stopped waiting for some far-off moment to feel joy. I stopped waiting for things to 'get better'. I stopped waiting for the next season, the next week, the next year, and for the first time, I began to live fully, to *be* fully, in every moment.

I cherish the small things: the grey hairs that are starting to pepper my head, the wrinkles that speak of laughter and love, the hands that continue to hold, the legs that carry me forward. I've learnt to see these as treasures. They are reminders of all I've survived, all I've overcome and all I still have to give. I no longer wait for the perfect moment. I've stopped waiting for happiness to come as if it were something to be earned. Happiness isn't a distant shore; it's something that blooms here and now, in the soil of today's struggles and in the cracks of tomorrow's promises. It's a choice; it's mine, and it's yours, too.

So, don't believe anyone who tells you your twenties are your only 'golden years'. Don't let anyone convince you that life is over once you've reached a certain age or that happiness is only meant for the lucky few. All of life is a golden opportunity. Every moment holds the potential for abundance, for change, for growth. You only have to be willing to meet it halfway. The journey from surviving to thriving isn't linear. It doesn't follow the path you expect, but it's worth it. The years I spent rediscovering myself have been worth every tear, every setback, every doubt. Through it all, I learnt that the true work of healing is not about fixing something broken; it's about realising that we are already whole.

This was my chance to take full responsibility for the life I've always wanted, and I've come to believe that we are all given that same opportunity if only we have the courage to take it.

There is no 'right' moment. There is only *now*, the chance to change, to transform, to embrace the truth that we are more than the limitations of our circumstances. We are not bound by time or pain. We are bound only by our own beliefs about what's possible. If we are willing to open our minds and hearts, we will find that there are no limits to what we can create, no boundaries to the love and light we can bring into the world.

You can change your life. You can make it brighter, more beautiful, more meaningful, but it starts with one thing: *the energy you bring to each moment.* The only way out of the darkness is to go inward, to reconnect with the part of you that knows no fear, no doubt, no limitation because we are not just bodies moving through time; we are eternal souls connected to the vastness of the universe.

When we face death—whether it's the death of a loved one or the death of who we used to be—the ego has no power over us. We are free. We are pure consciousness, untouchable by fear, untouched by time. In that moment, we remember what we have always known: life is not about surviving; it is about deeply knowing that we are part of something far greater than ourselves.

Death, in its deepest truth, is not the end; it is the opportunity of a lifetime, a chance to understand the mystery of existence, to step into the light of pure consciousness, to shed what isn't ours and to remember who we truly are.

As I stand here at the end of one chapter and the beginning of another, I know that life will keep unfolding, and I will keep walking with my flowers in hand, with love in my heart, and with a soul that will never stop growing.

At that moment, I realised we've been looking at life and death all wrong. We've been hypnotised by a distorted, fearful view of death, a view that traps us in terror and grief, as if it's something to fear or avoid. We've been taught to see death as an end, but I now see it as the very essence of life itself. Without death, there can be no life, and without life, death would not have its place. Death isn't the enemy; it is the key that unlocks the truth we've been searching for. It reveals what cannot be manipulated or distorted by fear, by ego, by anything that tries to control us. Death leads us back to ourselves, to the core of who we are.

So, I came to understand that my loved ones — those who are no longer physically with us — are not gone. They are alive in the memories, in the lessons, in the love they left behind. They are still here inside of me, around me, a part of the energy that makes up everything I touch and everything I am.

When we face death, we face freedom. The ultimate freedom, the kind that only comes when we let go of everything we thought we knew. That, to me, is extraordinary freedom. It's a freedom that transforms grief from a thief of joy to a teacher of truth. In that moment of realisation, I knew, with all my heart, that grief would no longer steal my joy. I chose to live from a place of energy, of presence, of truth, and in doing so, I set myself free — forever.

If you've ever lost someone you loved or if life hasn't turned out as you expected, I want you to know this: you are not alone in your pain. I hope this book serves as a guide to help you find your strength again, just as it helped me find mine. What I've learnt—what I want you to understand—is this: your perspective on everything big and small is the key to your reality. It's your perspective that shapes the world you live in, and it's your perspective that determines your happiness.

If you've ever wondered if you are worthy of a beautiful life, if you've ever questioned your place in this vast, mysterious world, I want you to remember this simple truth: You are worthy simply because you exist. You would not exist if you were not meant to be here if you did not have something unique and irreplaceable to offer the world. Your existence is not pointless. You are a vital part of the grand puzzle, and the world needs you just as you are.

Spend your life loving, not seeking love. Spend your life happy, not chasing happiness. Too many of us search for the 'right' person, the 'right' job, the 'right' circumstances, but how many of us stop and ask, 'Am I the right person?' Life is not a rehearsal; it is the one shot we get to be fully, unapologetically ourselves.

Existence is not about gain or competition, victory or failure. The purpose of life is not in the things we accumulate or the titles we wear. The purpose is to know who we truly are, to live in a way that honours our deepest truths, and love—the kind of love that transcends fear, that connects us to each other and to the universe.

When I met my authenticity again, when I finally recognised the truth of who I was, everything became clearer. I was no longer a shadow of myself, a reflection of someone I thought I should be. I was me, in all my raw, imperfect glory. My voice, once so small and uncertain, now resonated loudly and vibrantly in the world.

In finding myself, I'd lost so much. I lost the illusions, the misconceptions, the comfort of hiding behind a false sense of self, but it wasn't a loss at all—it was a shedding, a beautiful, liberating shedding of everything that wasn't truly mine. In that loss came the most beautiful gifts: my voice, my self-expression, my clarity, my creativity, my boundaries, my imagination, my purpose. I thought I couldn't lose anything else after my brother, but what I gained in the process of losing my false self was something far more powerful: I found my truth. And in finding my truth, I discovered that loss is not an end. It is simply a beginning, another step in the journey of remembering who we are, why we're here, and what it means to truly live.

When you find yourself searching for magic, convinced that it must exist somewhere in the world—somewhere out there, waiting to be discovered—remember this:

magic is not something outside of you. You won't ever catch it by chasing it or looking for it in the far corners of the Earth. Magic isn't a thing you can hold or possess—it is you. It lives inside you. If you live so authentically that others call you delusional, so be it. That's just the language of those who don't understand what it means to be alive with purpose, to walk in faith, and to create beauty from the heart.

So, wherever you are—whether you live in the sunshine or in the rain—live in the light of your own truth. Even in the darkest, stormiest days, don't forget that you have the power to create a space where the pressure of the rain can forge diamonds. The challenges are not your curse; they are your making, and in those moments, you are becoming everything you were always meant to be.

One day, you'll let your life become more than you ever thought it could be, and when you do, you'll hear that little calling in your heart, the one that becomes your purpose, your true north. One day, it will click, and you'll realise that life has been waiting for you to step into a version of yourself so expansive, so limitless, that you couldn't have even imagined it before. There are others, just like you, taking huge leaps in the direction you always dreamed of. The only difference between them and you is that they chose to take that leap. Now, it's your turn.

It's time to begin projecting yourself into the world, not just in the places where you're seen but in the quiet, unspoken moments. Love isn't something you just feel or give—it is something you are. Love should pulse through you in all your relationships, in every interaction, in every word, and even in the moments when you're alone. Love is in your gratitude, in your thoughts, in the quiet habits of your everyday life. Love is infinite and boundless, and though some may fear it, avoid it, or even settle for distance because they're afraid of being burned, the truth is this: love is the bravest thing you can do. Love with all of your breath, and watch as it breathes new life into you.

It doesn't matter what happened a day ago, a week ago, a month ago or even years ago. Nothing is permanent unless you choose to make it so. So, be gentle with the person you are today. Look at all you've done to become who you are right now. Every step you've taken, every tear, every triumph, every lesson—it's all brought you to this moment, and you wouldn't be here without every version of yourself that came before. Don't ever give up on the journey because every choice you make today is the chance to change your tomorrow.

Life is not about accumulating things or titles; it's about being a collector of experiences, not being defined by them but being enriched by them, learning from them, growing through them and sharing them. Look back, not with regret, but with awe. See the beauty in the blissful mundanity of life and realise it was a privilege to have lived it.

Fall wildly back in love with your life. Let it be messy, beautiful, unpredictable and bold. I hope, one day, you can look at your life and say, 'I chose this life. I didn't settle for it. I embraced it, I created it, and I am living it fully,' and when you do, you'll know that the most magical thing of all is simply this: you are the magic.

Definitions

Abundance: The freedom to effortlessly accomplish what needs to be done, exactly when it's required.

Awareness: A realisation of possibilities that were previously outside of your conscious consideration.

Belief: A thought that you continuously reinforce, shaping your reality and actions.

Consciousness: The deep awareness of how your thoughts and emotions shape your perception of the world.

Ego: The self-constructed sense of identity, perceived as separate from all else in existence.

Electromagnetic Field: A dynamic energy field created when electrical (thoughts) and magnetic (feelings) charges interact.

Emotions: The flow of energy that moves through you, shaping your inner experience.

Energy: Wherever your attention goes, your energy flows—shaping the world around you.

Entanglement: A phenomenon where particles remain interconnected, with changes in one instantaneously affecting the other, regardless of distance. It's a reminder that everything is interconnected; we are all one.

Fifth Dimension (5D): A subjective realm where your thoughts, emotions, and energy shape your personal reality. It's unique to each individual, with your consciousness influencing the circumstances, people, and experiences that resonate with your inner state. In the 5D, you create your reality through the frequency you emit.

Human Consciousness: The awareness of your existence as a unique expression of Source Consciousness within the physical world. It involves being present, perceiving external realities, and experiencing internal thoughts, emotions, and sensations.

Inspiration: The divine guidance that stirs creativity and insight, often perceived as coming from a higher source.

Manifest: The process of bringing thoughts, beliefs, and emotions together to create tangible outcomes in your life.

Matter: A physical substance that occupies space and can be measured.

Mind: The active processing centre of the brain, where thoughts and perceptions arise.

Mirror of Reality: The concept that the world reflects back to you the state of your own being.

Self-Forgiveness: The unconditional release of anger, resentment, and the need for punishment—both for yourself and others—freeing you from past offenses, flaws, and mistakes.

Self-Concept (State of Being): The collective beliefs, thoughts, and feelings—both conscious and subconscious—that define who you believe yourself to be.

Subconscious Mind: The automatic part of your mind that stores and processes information without your active awareness, influencing your behaviour and decisions.

Third Dimension (3D): The physical realm of solid matter, defined by its slower rate of vibration, where we experience our everyday lives.

Unconsciousness: A state in which awareness is absent, and the capacity to perceive or respond is lost.

Victim: The mindset of avoiding responsibility by constantly seeking external reasons for personal hardships.

Vibrational Shift: A transformative change in one's energy and state of being, marking a transition toward a higher level of consciousness, growth, and personal evolution.

Quantum Field: An unseen realm of energy and intelligence that transcends time and space, governing the laws of nature and encompassing all possible outcomes.

About the Author

Rania's passion for literature began in childhood, when her innate love for books sparked a deep, lifelong fascination with storytelling. As a young girl, she even crafted handmade books from cardboard, proudly calling herself an author. As she matured, writing became intricately intertwined with her studies in Law.

In April 2016, a life-changing event left her devastated, and writing was far from her thoughts.

Though a professional career took precedence in her twenties, an inner voice continually reminded her that ignoring her creative side was at odds with her true nature.

After years of healing and self-discovery, a spark of creativity was reignited. Recognising that it was time to write again, she poured her heart into '*I CAN, YOU CAN*'—a book born from her own journey. The book aims to help others transform emotional and mental struggles into lives filled with happiness, limitless possibility, and extraordinary self-belief.

www.rania-habib.com

Conscious Dreams
PUBLISHING

Transforming diverse writers
into successful published authors

www.consciousdreamspublishing.com

authors@consciousdreamspublishing.com

Let's connect

www.ingramcontent.com/pod-product-compliance
Ingram Content Group UK Ltd.
Pitfield, Milton Keynes, MK11 3LW, UK
UKHW021127090625
6296UKWH00038B/409

9 781917 584326